Brief Strategic Solution-Oriented Therapy of Phobic and Obsessive Disorders

GIORGIO NARDONE

FOREWORD BY PAUL WATZLAWICK
PREFACE BY ALESSANDRO SALVINI

JASON ARONSON INC.
Northvale, New Jersey
London

The author gratefully acknowledges permission to reprint material from:

Diagnostic and Statistical Manual of Mental Disorders, 4th ed. (*DSM-IV*). Copyright © 1994 by the American Psychiatric Association.

"La Paura è semplicemente un'emozione?" by A. Salvini, in *Rivista di Scienze Sessuologiche* 4(1):9–16. Copyright © 1991 by Alessandro Salvini.

This book was set in 11 pt. Berkeley by Alpha Graphics of Pittsfield, New Hampshire, and printed and bound by Book-mart Press of North Bergen, New Jersey.

Library of Congress Cataloging-in-Publication Data

Nardone, Giorgio.
    Brief strategic solution-oriented therapy of phobic and obsessive
disorders / Giorgio Nardone ; foreword by Paul Watzlawick ;
preface by Alessandro Salvini
        p.   cm.
    Includes bibliographical references and index.
    ISBN 1-56821-804-4
    1. Phobias—Treatment.   2. Obsessive-compulsive disorder—
Treatment.   3. Strategic therapy.   4. Solution-focused therapy.
I. Title.
    [DNLM: 1. Phobic Disorders—therapy.   2. Psychotherapy, Brief
methods.   3. Obsessive-Compulsive Disorder—therapy.   4. Panic
Disorder—therapy.   WM 178 N224b   1996]
RC535.N378   1996
616.85'22506—dc20
DNLM/DLC
for Library of Congress   95-52096

Printed in the United States of America on acid-free paper. For information and catalog write to Jason Aronson Inc., 230 Livingston Street, Northvale, New Jersey 07647. Or visit our website: http:/ /www.aronson.com

The characteristic aspect of panic fear lies in not clearly understanding its clauses, supposing them rather than knowing them, and in finally allowing fear itself to become a cause of fear.

Arthur Schopenhauer

Fear is like a too-short blanket: whichever way you pull, it always leaves some part of you uncovered.

Peter Weir

Contents

PART ONE:
THE TECHNIQUE OF BRIEF STRATEGIC
SOLUTION-ORIENTED THERAPY

PART TWO:
CASE EXAMPLES

Foreword

I am sincerely pleased to introduce a work which I consider to be a fundamental contribution in that it presents a constructivist-cybernetic model of the formation and persistence of human problems based on fear that provides the groundwork for future studies in this field, and describes strategies that have proved to be particularly efficient in changing and resolving such problems. Readers who are acquainted with Giorgio Nardone's previous works will not be surprised to find that here again he offers important contributions from both a theoretical and practical point of view.

The book begins with an account of what the author defines as a research-intervention on severe forms of fear, panic, and phobia. This section clearly shows the rigor and creativeness of Nardone's method, as he often "invents" original therapeutic "realities." The theoretical statements and therapeutic strategies presented here are the result of an experimental and empirical study of interventions on over 150 cases. Thus, we are not presented here with theories construed from the analysis of a single clinical case, as often happens in the field of psychotherapy.

In line with modern constructivist epistemology ("If you desire to see, learn how to act"), the method of inquiry by which the author studies the clinical problems connected with disorders based on fear is founded upon the construct "Know a Problem by Its Solution." In other words, knowledge of a reality is gained through the strategies that can change it and, thereby, reveal its functioning.

In conducting this strategic study, Nardone has concerned himself with *how* disorders based on fear function in their persistence, rather than with *why* such problems occur. Instead of leading patients to insight and awareness of the origins of their problems, his work has concentrated on their attempted dysfunctional solutions, that is, on the maneuvers that patients employ with the intention of fighting their fear, but with the opposite effect of complicating the fear instead of alleviating it. It is particularly interesting to observe how the author has been able to identify specific attempted dysfunctional solutions for different forms of phobic problems, and to show that if we succeed in making the patients change such dysfunctional and redundant ways of reacting to fear, the problems almost magically vanish. This result is achieved through apparently simple interventions such as refined suggestions, paradoxes, and behavioral tricks that lead patients to change their manner of experiencing and perceiving reality.

Along the same lines of thought, Nardone has devised specific strategies that facilitate quick and effective solutions to the different variants of phobic problems. These strategies are a synthesis of personal inventiveness, flexibility, and methodological rigor. The interventions require specific procedures in a certain order, and they need to be adapted to the individual patient's specific relational contexts. The two fully transcribed case examples in the Appendix show that, to be really effective, the methodical procedure must be adapted to the patient's language and perceptual framework. One must, likewise, be able to change the procedure whenever there is a change in therapeutic goals and interaction. The adaptiveness and strategic flexibility that distinguish this model of brief therapy show that it has the quality, in line with Gregory Bateson's thinking, of a system of rules with the property of self-correction. That is a rare feature among models of psychotherapy.

Finally, the results, measured in terms of the efficacy of a treatment applied to the great number of subjects presented here, are, to say the least, surprisingly positive, especially compared with the results usually obtained by classical forms of psychotherapy in treating the complicated problems in question.

In short, this book will be very useful to professionals in this field. I also recommend the book to anyone interested in the evolution of therapy based on systemic and constructivist theories; and since its language is clear and comprehensible, I feel that it can also be recommended to nonprofessional readers who may be fascinated with this topic and pleased to see that complicated, long-lasting, and painful problems such as the severest forms of fear do not necessarily require equally complicated, long-lasting, and painful solutions.

Paul Watzlawick
Palo Alto, California
July 1996

Preface

Perhaps the best way to present a book is to lead readers to appreciate its most notable features without trying to supplant their own judgment. The presentation should not be a rite in which the author and the presenter conspire behind the reader's back to give each other mutual luster, but rather a preliminary writing with useful considerations for understanding what follows.

The subject of this book is the strategic-constructivist approach to treating phobic-obsessive disorders, a therapeutic model and technique developed by Giorgio Nardone, and successfully applied to a variegated phenomenology of phobic disorders—in other words, the particular class of psychological problems that are manifested in pathological forms of fear.

The model that the author has tested and proposed here is a collection of techniques by which the therapist produces a change in the relational, cognitive, and emotional organization that underlies simple and generalized phobias. One distinguishing quality of this therapeutic method is that treatments are brief, and this makes it possible to immediately evaluate their efficacy. The therapist strives to extinguish the patient's symptoms and psychological distress. The therapist's strategies focus on reframing the patient's representations (and perceptions) of self, others, and the world—

in other words, the relational patterns that sustain and validate the patient's phobic perceptions.

This aim is simple, but it is difficult to reach. The proposed model has the virtue of clarity, conciseness, and controllability of procedures and results. The therapist and his techniques have no alibi; they either work or they don't, and everyone, including patients, can see the results and either be satisfied or not. That is a remarkable step forward for psychotherapy, which has the reputation of being a methodology that can never be disproved, not even by its clients, as the sole authority establishing right and wrong is the therapist with a thousand sophisms. It is for this reason that those psychologists who are most familiar with all the tricks and problems of science have scarce consideration for psychotherapies, and particularly for psychoanalysis.

The change that brief strategic-constructivist therapy is able to accomplish involves quickly, effectively, and attestably breaking down the cognitive and emotional patterns by which the patient's perception of self and model of relating to the disorder are organized—patterns that also provide the premise for resistances to change and for the permanence of the disorder to be alleviated. The techniques devised by Nardone and presented in this book have the pragmatic aim of disarranging the patient's solutions and adaptations, whose behavioral redundancies, functional to a defense against fear, have created a true homeostatic equilibrium.

This book does more than describe the model and give detailed explanations of the utilized techniques. The videorecorded and transcribed case examples give the reader a direct demonstration of how the models and techniques are applied. If it is true that we learn by doing, interested readers thus also become participants in a learning process—an engaging arrangement.

According to the strategic approach, a good therapist is also a good teacher. If he can succeed in adopting a patient's frame of reality and mental processes as his own, then when he is writing or teaching he will not neglect his readers' or listeners' point of view. He will accordingly make the learning process easier by exerting such manipulating, engaging, or reorganizing influence on mental categories as is necessary to change perspectives and mental constructs.

By proposing that we read the case examples in a certain manner, Nardone's work encourages this way of learning. It would have been too great and too original an effort, not easily appreciated by all his readers, if he had organized his book and his relationship with its readers in accordance with his own techniques. On the other hand, it might have been useful to do so, because all readers have resistances proportional to how long and how strongly they have identified with other therapeutic approaches and their implicit worldviews, specific language, and underlying epistemological paradigms. The more closely psychologists or psychiatrists are affiliated with a certain therapeutic faith—quite independently of the obtained results—the more they will defend by that faith not just their professional identity but also their concept of self.

The purpose of this digression is to convey the fact that, to fully appreciate the theoretical premise of this book, some preliminary information (or formation) may be required. This will help "resistant" readers to place the book within a certain tradition of thought that, when known, will strongly diminish these readers' reluctance, misunderstandings, or equivocations.

The approach devised by Nardone is the most advanced result of the meeting between the traditions of Palo Alto and Phoenix. These traditions are frequently referred to in the book. The closest precursors of this approach are (1) the brief systemic-strategic therapy of the Mental Research Institute in Palo Alto, mainly known by the works of Watzlawick and Weakland with whom Nardone has studied and now collaborates, and (2) the technical solutions created by Milton Erickson in the context of so-called hypnosis without trance.

This book shows that, while maintaining its autonomy, Nardone's work is the most recent and innovative product of the systemic tradition. The contribution it makes should not be confused with the systemic branch of family therapy, from which it distances itself in terms of epistemology, theory, and therapeutic practice. The therapeutic method proposed in this book is much closer to the epistemology of Gregory Bateson than are other, more dated systemic approaches. We find it inspired by, and close to the "constructivist" Bateson who, *mutatis mutandis*, has found continuance in Paul Watzlawick, if only for their analogous cultural breadth and anthropological sensitivity. Such breadth of knowledge is not always found in certain conventional conventicles of therapists who have degraded the systemic heritage to a reductive office practice.

As I have already mentioned, many psychologists mistrust certain kinds of psychotherapy and are afraid of being discredited for concerning themselves with them. Other kinds of therapies are credited with applying knowledge, to varying degrees, or respecting, as much as possible, the rules of the scientific game, for example, transparency and public verification of results, and consistency between theoretical assumptions and therapeutic practice. Nardone's work has these characteristics.

In the strategic-constructivist approach we find (even if only in passing reference) many theoretical fragments that are entirely unexceptional in the light of new knowledge produced in many branches of psychology, for example by social cognition, by interactionism, by studies on common sense and their implicit personality theories, not to mention all the recent contributions from researchers involved in the study of self-perceptive processes and the self.

Another positive aspect of the strategic approach is that both the therapist and the model set carefully limited objectives for themselves. The objectives that the theory must serve are to provide the appropriate premises, "glue," and logical consistency to the therapist's actions. The therapist must discover how his patient's internal and external relational perceptive system is organized in order to successfully introduce within it those reframing techniques that will lead to a resolution of the patient's psychological problem.

Although the author's hypotheses and pragmatic explanations have many points in common with the knowledge that presently explains interactive behavior and its mechanisms (for example, how persuasion occurs, or how individuals deceive themselves), it is not up to him to construct a theory of mental processes and submit it to experimental verifications. If strategic therapists confer provisional validity, but no ontological statute, to their theoretical map (the map is not the territory), that is due to a constructivist choice. Part of the theory is completed by what the patients offer as their own worldview and conception and explanation of self, by their ways of dealing with their problems, and by the meanings they attribute to them. To understand this position, we need only refer to something that Bateson wrote many years ago, that ontology and epistemology cannot be separated in the natural history of human beings; our usually unconscious convictions about the surrounding world determine our ways of seeing and acting within this world, and our ways of feeling and acting determine our convictions on the nature of the world. Living man is thus a prisoner in a web of epistemological and ontological premises that, quite apart from their ultimate truth or falseness, are partially self-validated.

What we do, say, and think about ourselves, others, and the world produces concrete phenomena, from feelings to actions, from illusions to empirical representations of realities, from interactive patterns to convictions, and so on, to that particular class of phenomena that generate suffering under the form of symptoms, but which is only the fruit of the conception of meanings and behavioral habits constructed by the subject. Intentionality of action does not always imply an adequate level of consciousness; the phobic subject is a paradigmatic example.

The aim of strategic therapy is to work out changes in modalities by which people have constructed private and dysfunctional realities. If the therapist is to produce changes in these modalities of action or representation, he must try to adopt the patient's style and manners of thought as his own, in short, "learn to speak the patient's own language"; only then can the therapist utilize the patient's codes of meanings and resources. The premise is that the human mind is not passive, predetermined, or reactive, but active and constructive in most of its processes; that is, it produces the realities it is subjected to.

Nardone's work describes and proposes the sequences and strategies that may be adopted and tested in order to unseat the patient's interactive cognitive and behavioral patterns and related mechanisms of confirmatory retroaction. But also part of the proposal is an evaluation of the effectiveness of the method and strategies. It is difficult to quantify and compare the results of clinical applications of therapeutic techniques because the variables connected to the psychological disorder, to biographical-relational data, and to individual responses are not homogeneous and therefore are scarcely controllable, and many other variables, such as the famous "intervening" variables, are unknown.

However, Nardone has honestly and pragmatically taken the remission of symptoms as his quantitative indicator. The effectiveness of treatments can thus be evaluated through empirical data and a follow-up study, together with a well-supported presentation of the therapy in action in the case examples. Obviously, much of what the therapist does is part of the profession. The therapeutic "moves" are only apparently simple; they require ad hoc, contextual, individual, and original solutions. Beyond the treatment protocol, this aspect is not likely to be transmitted together with the package of instructions for use, nor should it be considered a residual variable with respect to the results and comparisons by which Nardone is asking us to evaluate the efficacy of the therapy.

This book is mainly about fear, about those kinds of apparently unmotivated, paralyzing, panic-filled, and anxiety-generating fears whose multiplicity and diversity is not sufficiently expressed by the nosological label classifying them as "phobias." The phobic organization of the personality involves how the individual acts, thinks, and imagines reality from a personal point of view that is also related to that individual's self-concept and the system of relationships of which he or she is part. Paradoxical as it may seem, phobic persons are not so much the result of something they have been subjected to as they are people who, despite themselves, prescribe their own problems. In other words, they are the actors who become anxious and fearful of their self-assigned roles, and the applause they receive from the public (concern and help from other people) only makes the patients' identification with pathological roles more credible, realistic, and truthful. Aside from theatrical metaphor, Nardone shows how patterns of self-representation and persisting relationships with the realities against which the phobic person is fighting indeed play important roles in determining the persistence of the disorder.

At this point, I will suspend this discussion on phobias and strategic modalities of treatment and leave it to the book itself. As Nardone is careful to point out, the term *phobia* is a linguistic expediency, a useful conventional label for conveying the complex phenomenology of a psychological problem. The phenomenon itself must not be confused with, or reduced to, the word that designates its symptom. But, as Herman Melville wrote about Billy Budd, when told without compromises, the truth will present confused boundaries.

Alessandro Salvini
Padua, Italy
July 1996

Introduction

THE STRUCTURE OF THIS BOOK

Everything is simpler than one would think, and at the same time more complicated than it is possible to understand.

Goethe

The expositive structure chosen for this book is meant to make it a synthesis between a purely scientific exposition with a detailed account of our studies and research, and an attractive exposition with quotations of anecdotes and metaphors in a style that makes it accessible to readers who are not experts in our field. I want to make it as readable as possible, while preserving the method and rigor that are necessary in an exposition of scientific constructs of theory and practice. This book is meant both for specialists, who will find in it a detailed description of an innovative theory on fear (its formation, persistence, and change) and for nonprofessionals who are interested in a problem of such great social relevance as the more severe forms of disorders based on fear.

The psychological and psychiatric literature has too often presented this problem as something unresolvable, or something that can be reduced only through many years of costly and laborious psychotherapy. On the contrary, the fact that a problem is complicated, long-standing, and has a cruel symptomatology does not mean that it needs an equally complicated, long-lasting, and torturing treatment in order to be resolved.

In other words, I also hope this book can inform the public about innovative and efficacious forms of intervention for problems that too often remain unresolved for years, not because of something inherent in the problems, but because of the inefficacy of therapeutic interventions carried out on them.

Toward those ends, this exposition will begin with a presentation of data regarding the large sample of subjects who came to my clinic to be treated for phobic or obsessive-compulsive disorders. This will make it clear from the beginning that the statements about theory and practice found in this book are not the fruit of the nocturnal fantasies or the morning illuminations of the thinker-healer of the day; nor are the practical and theoretical constructs based on a single clinical case or on too small a sample of cases (unfortunately a very frequent procedure in our field).

In this presentation, I will also explain how the work that made it possible to prepare this model of treatment developed over time. Thus, I will describe my formulations, hypotheses, and the procedures that are utilized to study, test, and prepare specific intervention techniques and their most appropriate order of application.

Chapter 2 presents the theoretical and practical formulations that emerged from this research intervention on how severe disorders based on fear are formed and how they persist, owing to the perceptions and consequent reactions of the subjects and their families and friends.

Chapter 3 gives a detailed presentation of the treatment protocol, the final result of the research intervention, in its several variants, composed of specific therapeutic techniques and their appropriate temporal sequences.

Chapter 4 presents the outcome, in terms of effectiveness, of the application of this form of intervention on a sample of 152 subjects.

Chapter 5 presents a comparison of the distinguishing features of several traditional models of therapy for phobic disorders and the model presented in this book, emphasizing both the characteristics that they have in common and their divergences in theory and practice. The Epilogue deals in a rather paradoxical way with the problem of when the type of treatment described throughout this book might not be advisable. The Appendix is a complete transcription of the videorecordings of two therapies, with each move pointed out in the heading to each section.

CYBERNETIC-CONSTRUCTIVIST EPISTEMOLOGY:
TO KNOW A PROBLEM BY ITS SOLUTION

The present work is, primarily, the report of an empirical research experience in clinical field. After repeated experimentations, this study led to the development of a psychotherapeutic model that makes it possible to resolve the problems connected with severe forms of fear, panic, and phobia quickly and effectively. Based on the research-intervention method, and applied to over 150 subjects in six years, this study also turned out to be a surprisingly good instrument for acquiring operative knowledge about phobic-obsessive disorders. The data gathered by our research staff made it possible to develop a model of knowledge and treatment of the formation, persistence, and resolutive change of phobic disorder typologies.

A clinical endeavor whose objective was the speedy and effective solution of the patients' problem thus made it possible to gather information that opened up new perspectives on the problems we were treating. In other words, a study that was geared toward the development of efficacious interventions also made it possible to acquire more, and sometimes innovative, information regarding the disorder typologies that were the subject of the intervention.

Our method of research-intervention is in line with Lewinian ideas on psychosocial research-action and concepts of change and stasis. As Festinger has remarked, one of Lewin's most important contributions to psychosocial thought is the idea of

> studying things by changing them and observing the effects. The idea that, to understand exactly how a process works, one must create a change and observe its variable effects and new dynamics is found throughout Lewin's work and is still extremely pertinent. [Amerio 1982, p. 189]

Working on that assumption, which also seems in line with modern constructivist epistemology (Foerster 1970, 1973, 1974, 1987, Glasersfeld 1979, 1984, 1995), we have come to know a reality by operating on it, gradually adjusting our interventions by adapting them to the new elements of knowledge that were emerging.

Following the prescriptions of second-order theorists (Foerster, Keeney), we studied both the observed and the observing systems, with particular attention to the interaction between these two systems and the effect of this interaction on our objective of resolving the patient's problem.

This study, or research-intervention as we prefer to call it, allowed us to prepare a specific treatment protocol that is particularly efficacious with phobic-obsessive disorders. It also gave us more knowledge of the reality on which we were intervening, or, as we define it, of the "perceptive-reactive" system of persons suffering from severe forms of phobic disorders.

For all these reasons, our exposition is not only about the change and solution but also about the formation and persistence of the problem of fear. We do not claim that the practical and theoretical constructs presented here form a definitive theory of fear, because as clinicians and therapists, we have, in the course of our observations, utilized a particular "lens" that belongs only to the therapeutic context.

According to contemporary epistemology, any kind of knowledge that is established in the interactive process between therapist and patient is the product of the particular invented reality that is the therapeutic inter-action. From observing one context, we cannot draw any theory that does not exclusively refer to that context. Otherwise, we would be in the same epistemological error that unfortunately most psychological and psychi-atric theorizations based on clinical studies fall into—that of arbitrarily transferring knowledge based on clinical experience to nonclinical con-texts, which would be as incorrect as an ethologist making observations on wild animal behavior on the basis of observations of domestic animal behavior.

The fact that, in our case, the invented reality that exists between therapist and patient during therapy was observed in a great number of cases and resulted in tangible changes in the patients' personal reality out-side the therapeutic context cannot be considered an epistemologically valid criterion of knowledge about any context outside the clinical one, such as the interaction between the individual and reality.

The clinical situation is thus a partial observation point of any reality, in our case, with respect to fear, panic, and phobia. What we can expect from our study, research, and experimentation within this partial context is, at best, purely operative knowledge, or what Glaserfeld would refer to as "operative consciousness." From our point of view, therefore, the prac-tical and theoretical constructs that are presented in this book should be seen not as theories of knowledge that describe the existential essence of fear, panic, and phobia, but only as technical knowledge and constructs, that is, models that allow us to prepare ever more effective techniques for the solution of the problems they are applied to, or for reaching our pre-established goals.

Besides, as Bateson said, in perfect harmony with modern philosophy of science (Popper 1968, 1972, 1973), the task of science is not to build perfect theoretical castles, but to devise efficacious intervention techniques based on goals.

Consequently, what we declare to be the precautional limitation of our work (the inability to describe the phenomenon of fear with its complex expressions in human realities exhaustively, focusing only on devising and preparing effective ad hoc strategies for the problems presented by patients) paradoxically becomes a great merit, since it awards scientific status to our work and represents a criterion for epistemological correctness.

A BRIEF CHRONOLOGICAL HISTORY
OF THE RESEARCH INTERVENTION

Real truths are the kind that can be invented.

Karl Kraus

Early in my career, a gentleman who had a desperate history of fears and obsessions that had persecuted him for years came into my office. He interpreted any minimal change in his bodily sensations as clear signs that he had caught an "obscure disease." He never went out alone for fear of feeling sick. He interpreted anything that he read or heard on television about various kinds of diseases as applying to himself; this used to throw him into a state of anguished panic. After years of pharmaceutical treatments, psychoanalysis, and magic cures attempted by witches, seers, and several religious people, this person had now turned to me.

I asked him why he had come to me, a young and inexperienced therapist, after having tried so many other treatments. I said that, considering how complicated his problem was, and how small my experience, there was very little I could do to help him. Our first session was spent in an atmosphere of pessimism and discouragement, with him telling me all his troubles and me repeatedly declaring how small his chances of recovery were and above all my total disillusion as to what might I be able to do for him.

When I saw him again after a week, I found an altogether changed person in front of me. Calm and smiling, the man announced that in the previous few days he had not experienced any of those great problems; he more than ever wanted to construct a new life for himself on the basis of this newfound state of health and psychological energy. Even more surprised than he, I tried to understand how this could have occurred, and made him tell me what had happened during that week.

After leaving my office, the patient had felt very depressed and discouraged and longing to end it all. He had already attempted suicide several times in the past. In the following days, his thoughts about suicide had progressively increased. He told me that for two or three days he kept thinking about what his life would be like without any hope of recovering from his disorders, and on this wave of desperation he actively thought about how to do away with himself. After discarding the already-attempted strategies (drug poisoning, car accident) he decided, perhaps because he lived close to the railway, to throw himself under a train.

Thus, as the patient described it, when the sun was about to disappear from the horizon, he lay down on the railroad tracks thinking about the ugliest things in the world and waiting for the "liberating" passage of the train. Oddly, at that moment he could only see the possible beauty of existence. While lying there waiting for the train, he began to see existence in a positive light, to the point of entering a state of deep relaxation and surrendering to mental images of a possible happy existence, free from his terrible symptoms. Suddenly the sound of an approaching train woke him from that pleasurable state. For a moment, he was almost surprised to be there; then he jumped off the tracks before the train arrived. He had returned to reality. He realized that he had been waiting to commit suicide; as if by magic, he was now seeing things in a new way, and feeling like another person, someone who no longer had any intention of dying.

After that, the fears in his mind disappeared as if by magic, and he started going out, looking for the friends he had abandoned in the isolation of his disorder. He no longer felt those terrifying symptoms clinging to him. He felt a strong wish to live, and began to look for a job (he had been unemployed because of his disorder).

I continued to see this patient for a few months, assisting in his gradual, progressive evolution toward a life without fears and obsessions and his complete reintegration in affective and professional life.

The case of this man completely upset the concepts of therapy I held at the time. According to traditional concepts of psychotherapy, it seemed unthinkable that such a sudden and quick recovery could have occurred. To me this experience was a kind of "enlightenment."

Earlier readings of Milton Erickson's work came to mind; at the time, I had thought of them as shamanistic accounts, not rigorous therapies. The idea that now formed strongly in my mind was that it would be wonderful to be able to deliberately provoke sudden changes such as this fortuitous one by systematically constructed interventions. Practically speaking, I began to think about how much I would have liked to study possibilities of intervening in so-called psychopathologies in such a way as to provoke quick and effective changes, as if by magic.

With these ideas in my head, I started reading Erickson's works carefully again. I found that his methods, which at first reading might not seem very systematic, actually had refined strategic constructions and decidedly systematic tactical structures.

I also found the same strategic refinement and tactical methodicity even more rigorously studied in the light of modern epistemology and research in human sciences in the works of Watzlawick, Weakland, and their colleagues at the Palo Alto school.

In short, thanks to that fortuitous and surprising case of sudden recovery, my conceptions opened up toward innovative perspectives on the formation and solution of human problems. One thing that became clear to me by closely studying the works of the Palo Alto group was that a concordance between the epistemological studies of the natural sciences and those of the psychological and social sciences was possible. Until then, this concept had seemed decidedly unsustainable in the light of comparisons between the research methods of physical and natural sciences and the traditional concepts in psychotherapy.

Another interesting patient came to see me shortly thereafter. She was a woman suffering from panic and agoraphobic disorders, who for a few years had been unable to leave her home without company; she was also unable to stay at home alone without falling prey to panic.

Since it was a very hot day, I got up from my chair and went to open the window. As I moved the curtain, the curtain rod became dislodged and fell noisily on my head, hitting me with its sharp end. At first I tried to downplay this accident by making a joking remark. I then sat down again, continuing my session with the patient. But I saw her become pale, and then felt the blood running down my head. I stood up, tried to calm her with another joking remark, and went to the bathroom. Looking in the mirror I realized how serious my wound was. I walked back into the office and told the patient that I needed to go to the emergency room for treatment. The patient immediately offered to take me, and forgetting that she had not driven a car for several years due to her phobia, she drove my car all the way to the hospital. When we got there, still forgetful of her fear, she watched, without flinching, the whole medical procedure including disinfection and suture of the stitches, assuming a protective and reassuring role toward me.

We returned to my office, where her husband, who had meanwhile come to fetch her, was astonished to see her calmly driving a car. But he was even more surprised to hear about her behavior during this incident. Considering her long-term problems with fear, it seemed not merely surprising but close to miraculous.

That was not the end of surprises for her husband. In the next few days, his wife began to go out alone, calmly driving her car and gradually resuming many activities that she had abandoned because of her fears. Only a few more sessions of gradual and progressive guided exploration and exposition to previously anxiety-laden situations were needed before she had completely overcome her phobic symptomatology.

As the reader can easily understand, this curious, fortuitous episode gave me much cause for reflection; it made me think about how nice it would be to be able to produce tangible experiences similar to this one by giving patients deliberate prescriptions under suggestion, producing events that could make the patients experience alternative modalities of perception and reaction toward reality and thus gently lead them to overcome their problems.

From then on, my studies and applications in the clinical field focused on the experimental study and preparation of strategic interventions of that kind—brief forms of treatment constructed on the basis of preestablished objectives that could lead the subjects to change almost without realizing it. But to do this, I had to emancipate myself completely from traditional concepts of psychotherapy. I needed to draw on other sources, on studies on human change, interaction, and communication. This study and research brought me into direct contact, in the role of an "apprentice," with the Mental Research Institute at Palo Alto, in particular with Paul Watzlawick, who showed me that, in the light of concrete clinical experiences and innovative forms of epistemology, it was possible to construct, within the interaction among people, invented realities that had the power to produce concrete effects.[1]

Watzlawick and Weakland became the rigorous and encouraging supervisors of my project to study and prepare a specific protocol for the brief therapy of phobic-obsessive disorders. My study and clinical research on severe forms of fear, panic, and phobia thus began to take form. My choice of dealing specifically with these clinical questions was due to several factors: (1) my dissatisfaction with the results obtained by traditional forms of psychotherapy; (2) a large number of phobic patients in my practice at the time, which was not accidental—despite all my protests that I had absolutely no responsibility for the changes, the two cases reported above had given me a great amount of publicity; and (3) while the Mental Research Institute model of brief therapy was being applied to disparate problems as an effect of its tradition of family and systemic therapy, it appeared to be little applied to phobic-obsessive disorders. Likewise, other models of brief therapy with a systemic basis did not appear to be specifically used for phobic disorders (de Shazer 1982, 1985, 1994). But Erickson's works contained many examples of brief and strategic intervention for serious forms of phobia and obsessions. This line of research, therefore, not only had the appeal of the therapist's becoming, perhaps, a powerful healer of severe forms of psychological symptomatology, but also contained aspects of novelty and originality that increased my enthusiasm.

The first thing I did was to equip my office, in the classical manner of Bateson's systemic researchers, with a closed-circuit videocamera and an observation room. I began to record my meetings with the phobic patients on whom I applied the Mental Research Institute model of brief therapy with some personal modifications and initial adaptations. After the sessions, I would review the therapeutic interaction, its development, and its effects, paying particular attention to the therapeutic maneuvers and communication utilized.

I started eliminating the maneuvers observed to be inefficacious and repeating those that seemed to produce changes in the patients. This ex-

---

1. The relationship with Watzlawick and his colleagues has evolved since then, from the original teacher–student relationship to one of collaboration and exchange of research. This collaboration has led to the publication of *The Art of Change* (Nardone and Watzlawick 1993).

perimentation was the leading motif of my research-intervention work on phobic disorders. Indeed, it was my success or lack of success at provoking changes and my consequent readjustments that led to the discovery of how certain dysfunctional human systems function in their problematical existence, and how it is possible to resolve such problems effectively.

The first three years of this work were a continuous experimentation either with techniques borrowed from many different therapeutic approaches, or with entirely invented ones that I thought might be useful. Each therapeutic maneuver was studied and analyzed with the aim of finding its most efficacious articulation and modality of communication. It soon became clear that it would not only be useful to have specific procedures for specific problems, but also that having a specific sequence for the treatment process would increase the intervention power of the maneuvers and lead more effectively to the preestablished objectives (Nardone and Watzlawick 1993).

After three years' work, I had prepared a first version of a specific model of brief therapy for phobic and obsessive disorders, composed of a series of specific therapeutic procedures and processes. As in chess, the therapeutic process was articulated in successive phases. Each phase had specific objectives; for each objective, specific tactics and modalities of therapeutic communication had been studied and developed. A series of possible maneuvers to avoid some predictable resistances on the part of the patient were also studied.

By experimenting with the two initial forms of strategic protocol, we were able to prepare a model of intervention composed of a preestablished series of procedures, but also provided with flexibility. The model could be adapted to the specific therapeutic interaction. This model is analogous to what a chess player does when he tries to reach checkmate as soon as possible by planning certain moves and trying to predict his opponent's countermoves.

It was understandably necessary to carry out a patient and laborious empirical and experimental study of phobic patients' usual reactions to specific maneuvers before being able to prepare this treatment protocol, which in its successive applications proved to be not only efficient but also predictive and heuristic. Sometimes we had to construct specific techniques for achieving the goals established at the outset in each stage of the therapy.

The final result might be described as something similar to what checkmate in a few moves represents in chess. However, it soon became clear that in therapy, contrary to chess, where the game is cold and mathematical, the quality of the interpersonal relations between the therapist and the patient is a crucial factor in determining the final results. In this regard, the teachings of Erickson on the use of injunctive communication and those of Watzlawick on the use of paradox, double binds, and other teachings of communication science have been indispensable for the development of the strategic plans and the specific therapeutic techniques.

The model has two versions, one for disorders based on obsessions and the other for disorders based on phobias. It has now been applied to more than 200 subjects, although the cases considered in this research are only the 152 that have already been through follow-up, three months, six months, and one year after the end of therapy. The model is decidedly successful, with 86 percent positive results (median duration of therapy: fourteen sessions).

Thus the objective of preparing a systematic and rigorous model of therapy that would deliberately produce what had occurred accidentally in the two described cases was achieved. Within the therapeutic interaction, we are now able to construct an invented reality that can produce effects in the patients' day-to-day realities.

The therapist who carries out such interventions seems like the wandering sage of this Islamic story:

> At his death, Ali Baba left 39 camels to his four sons. His will provided that the inheritance should be divided in the following way: one half was to go to the eldest son, one quarter to the second, one eighth to the third, and to the youngest one tenth of the camels. The four brothers could not reach an agreement, and were in the middle of an animated discussion, when a wandering sage came riding by and, having been attracted by the dispute, intervened and resolved the brothers' problem in an almost magical way. He added his own camel to the 39 of the inheritance and started making the divisions under the puzzled looks of the brothers. He assigned 20 camels to the eldest son, 10 to the second, 5 to the third and 4 to the youngest. Then he mounted the remaining camel, considering that it was his own, and left again on his wanderings. [Eigen 1986, p. 140]

In his solution of the brothers' dilemma, the wandering sage added something that was indispensable to the solution, and then took it back, since it was no longer needed once the problem had been solved. Similarly, when we treat phobic patients we add something that is indispensable for the effective and speedy solution of the problem; but after the disorder has been overcome, we take that thing back because it is no longer necessary.

This type of intervention is only apparently "magic" because it is the fruit of the application of highly rigorous principles of problem solution. In their application, these principles provide for a creative adaptation to circumstances, so as to be able to break the "spells" represented by complicated and self-feeding human problems. For the rest, said Bateson (1979), "Rigor alone is death by paralysis, but imagination alone is folly" (p. 119).

Part I

The Technique
of Brief Strategic
Solution-Oriented Therapy

Defining the Problem and Methodologies

Everything that is believed in exists, and only that.

Hugo von Hofmannsthal

THE PROBLEM: DEFINITION AND DESCRIPTION OF SEVERE FORMS OF FEAR, PANIC, AND PHOBIA

The typologies of problems dealt with here need substantial explanation, because the terms *fear*, *panic*, and *phobia* are generally used to describe a great number of psychological and behavioral realities that, often due to different theories of reference, seem to have very little correspondence among each other.

> At a closer look, "fear" is a linguistic label by which we categorize different things according to our theoretical perspective and instruments of inquiry. Physical signals, facial expressions, behavioral traits and subjective experience will make any discourse upon fear become a discourse by an observer who constructs his "maps" by segmenting what he sees and placing it on different planes of reality. [Salvini 1991, p. 12]

For example, the same specific form of fear can be described: (1) by a psychoanalyst, as the effect of an unresolved childhood trauma; (2) by a behaviorist, as a form of learned behavior and social conditioning; (3) by a family therapist, as the product of a dysfunctional family relationship; (4) by a cognitivist, as a reaction to attachment and separation modalities; (5) by an existentialist, as an expression of the anxiety connected to "being in the world."

All these different perspectives remind us of the Indian metaphor about four blind men who were standing around an elephant. Each of them touched a different part of the elephant and stated that the part he touched was the "truth" of the elephant's constitution. The blind man who touched the trunk said that an elephant was something long and elastic, the man who touched the side said that an elephant was a mass of flesh, and so forth with other limited perceptions of the elephant's body.

From our point of view, that is, the strategic approach to the formation and solution of human problems (Nardone 1991, Nardone and Watzlawick 1993, Watzlawick et al. 1974), those kinds of distinctions are scarcely relevant, because they are only interpretations of the same problem typologies, and do not help us to devise efficacious solutions; they are often merely romanced or reductivist views of a problem.

If, on the contrary, we apply the premises of modern constructivist epistemology (Glaserfeld 1995), we will consider human problems as a product of the interaction between the subject and reality, and mainly of how each person perceives reality through the perspective, the instruments of knowledge and the kinds of language employed. This complex system of perception and elaboration of our selves, others, and the world constructs representations of realities that sometimes, in the case of people who suffer from a disorder, lead to dysfunctional responses. We define all this as a person's "perceptive-reactive" system.

We are interested here in how the problem functions in its dynamics and processes, in the study and discovery of the problem's particular rules and functions, and in the preparation of effective and quick solutions—in other words, with how the problem functions and not why the problem exists. This shift in attention allows us to concentrate on developing quick and effective solutions without wasting time on laborious, scarcely credible, and useless searches for the presumed causes of the present problem. From our perspective, problems are identified through empirical examination based on the statements made by the patients and their families and on what, during the interaction between the therapist and the patient, is defined as the problem to be resolved. In this research-intervention, therefore, severe phobic disorders are diagnosed directly on the basis of the patients' empirical reports; thus we avoid any form of interpretation of the data in our classification. The sample of subjects on which this study is based includes different typologies of problems based on fear, panic, or phobia.

A common trait of all our subjects is that they had become unable to lead autonomous lives, independent of their families and friends, and had lost the ability to carry out any activities on their own, free from fear or phobic fixations. These cases correspond to specific diagnostic classifications in the *DSM-IV*.

In our clinical work, we prefer to avoid the labels that are typical of psychiatric classification of psychological disorders and that lead to self-fulfilling prophecies about the labeled persons. In clinical practice, we deliberately use the word *problem* for its nonpathologizing connotations, instead of the word *disease*. To speak with our patients in terms of a problem rather than in terms of disease is to construct a therapeutic reality oriented toward solution; problems are made to be solved. For its depathologizing effect on the symptoms, this communicative maneuver of redefining disorders is often a proper therapeutic intervention.

In the context of this book, however, and for a methodological evaluation of our research-intervention, we should refer to a diagnostic classification of psychological disorders that is recognized by the international research community. Since this book is meant to contribute to discussion with other specialists, we will use terminology that we could not employ in the context of a clinical intervention.

After this explanation of our terminology, made necessary by the difference between the language of therapy (where communication is an instrument and a vehicle for intervention) and that of explanatory exposition (where communication is transmission of knowledge and experience) we quote the *DSM-IV* classification of the problems we have studied and treated.

Panic Attack

A discrete period of intense fear or discomfort, in which four (or more) of the following symptoms developed abruptly and reached a peak within 10 minutes:

(1) palpitations, pounding heart, or accelerated heart rate
(2) sweating
(3) trembling or shaking

(4) sensations of shortness of breath or smothering
(5) feeling of choking
(6) chest pain or discomfort
(7) nausea or abdominal distress
(8) feeling dizzy, unsteady, lightheaded, or faint
(9) derealization (feelings of unreality) or depersonalization (being detached from oneself)
(10) fear of losing control or going crazy
(11) fear of dying
(12) paresthesias (numbness or tingling sensations)
(13) chills or hot flushes. [p. 395]

Agoraphobia

A. Anxiety about being in places or situations from which escape might be difficult (or embarrassing) or in which help may not be available in the event of having an unexpected or situationally predisposed Panic Attack or panic-like symptoms. Agoraphobic fears typically involve characteristic clusters of situations that include being outside the home alone; being in a crowd or standing in line; being on a bridge; and traveling in a bus, train, or automobile.

Note: Consider the diagnosis of Specific Phobia if the avoidance is limited to one or only a few specific situations, or Social Phobia if the avoidance is limited to social situations.

B. The situations are avoided (e.g., travel is restricted) or else are endured with marked distress or with anxiety about having a Panic Attack or panic-like symptoms, or require the presence of a companion.

C. The anxiety or phobic avoidance is not better accounted for by another mental disorder, such as Social Phobia (e.g., avoidance limited to social situations because of fear of embarrassment), Specific Phobia (e.g., avoidance limited to a single situation like elevators), Obsessive-Compulsive Disorder (e.g., avoidance of dirt in someone with an obsession about contamination), Posttraumatic Stress Disorder (e.g., avoidance of stimuli associated with a severe stressor), or Separation Anxiety Disorder (e.g., avoidance of leaving home or relatives). [pp. 396–397]

Panic Disorder Without Agoraphobia

A. Both (1) and (2):

  (1) recurrent unexpected Panic Attacks (see above)
  (2) at least one of the attacks has been followed by 1 month (or
       more) of one (or more) of the following:
       (a) persistent concern about having additional attacks
       (b) worry about the implications of the attack or its conse-
            quences (e.g., losing control, having a heart attack, "going
            crazy")
       (c) a significant change in behavior related to the attacks.

B. Absence of Agoraphobia (see above).

C. The Panic Attacks are not due to the direct physiological effects of
    a substance (e.g., a drug of abuse, a medication) or a general medi-
    cal condition (e.g., hyperthyroidism).

D. The Panic Attacks are not better accounted for by another mental
    disorder, such as Social Phobia (e.g., occurring on exposure to
    feared social situations), Specific Phobia (e.g., on exposure to
    a specific phobic situation), Obsessive-Compulsive Disorder (e.g.,
    on exposure to dirt in someone with an obsession about con-
    tamination), Posttraumatic Stress Disorder (e.g., in response to
    stimuli associated with a severe stressor), or Separation Anxiety
    Disorder (e.g., in response to being away from home or close rela-
    tives). [p. 402]

Panic Disorder With Agoraphobia

A. Both (1) and (2):

  (1) recurrent unexpected Panic Attacks (see above)
  (2) at least one of the attacks has been followed by 1 month (or
       more) of one (or more) of the following:
       (a) persistent concern about having additional attacks
       (b) worry about the implications of the attack or its conse-
            quences (e.g., losing control, having a heart attack, "going
            crazy")
       (c) a significant change in behavior related to the attacks.

B. The presence of Agoraphobia (see above).

C. The Panic Attacks are not due to the direct physiological effects of a substance (e.g., a drug of abuse, a medication) or a general medical condition (e.g., hyperthyroidism).

D. The Panic Attacks are not better accounted for by another mental disorder, such as Social Phobia (e.g., occurring on exposure to feared social situations), Specific Phobia (e.g., on exposure to a specific phobic situation), Obsessive-Compulsive Disorder (e.g., on exposure to dirt in someone with an obsession about contamination), Post-traumatic Stress Disorder (e.g., in response to stimuli associated with a severe stressor), or Separation Anxiety Disorder (e.g., in response to being away from home or close relatives). [pp. 402–403]

Agoraphobia Without History of Panic Disorder

A. The presence of Agoraphobia (see above) related to fear of developing panic-like symptoms (e.g., dizziness or diarrhea).

B. Criteria have never been met for Panic Disorder (see above).

C. The disturbance is not due to the direct physiological effects of a substance (e.g., a drug of abuse, a medication) or a general medical condition.

D. If an associated general medical condition is present, the fear described in Criterion A is clearly in excess of that usually associated with the condition. [pp. 404–405]

Obsessive-Compulsive Disorder

A. Either obsessions or compulsions:

Obsessions as defined by (1), (2), (3), and (4):

(1) recurrent and persistent thoughts, impulses, or images that are experienced, at some time during the disturbance, as intrusive and inappropriate and that cause marked anxiety or distress
(2) the thoughts, impulses, or images are not simply excessive worries about real-life problems

(3) the person attempts to ignore or suppress such thoughts, impulses, or images, or to neutralize them with some other thought or action

(4) the person recognizes that the obsessional thoughts, impulses, or images are a product of his or her own mind (not imposed from without as in thought insertion).

Compulsions as defined by (1) and (2):

(1) repetitive behaviors (e.g., hand washing, ordering, checking) or mental acts (e.g., praying, counting, repeating words silently) that the person feels driven to perform in response to an obsession, or according to rules that must be applied rigidly

(2) the behaviors or mental acts are aimed at preventing or reducing distress or preventing some dreaded event or situation; however, these behaviors or mental acts either are not connected in a realistic way with what they are designed to neutralize or prevent or are clearly excessive.

B. At some point during the course of the disorder, the person has recognized that the obsessions or compulsions are excessive or unreasonable. **Note:** This does not apply to children.

C. The obsessions or compulsions cause marked distress, are time consuming (take more than 1 hour a day), or significantly interfere with the person's normal routine, occupational (or academic) functioning, or usual social activities or relationships.

D. If another Axis I disorder is present, the content of the obsessions or compulsions is not restricted to it (e.g., preoccupation with food in the presence of an Eating Disorder; hair pulling in the presence of Trichotillomania; concern with appearance in the presence of Body Dysmorphic Disorder; preoccupation with drugs in the presence of a Substance Use Disorder; preoccupation with having a serious illness in the presence of Hypochondriasis; preoccupation with sexual urges or fantasies in the presence of a Paraphilia; or guilty ruminations in the presence of Major Depressive Disorder).

E. The disturbance is not due to the direct physiological effects of a substance (e.g., a drug of abuse, a medication) or a general medical condition. [pp. 422–423]

We consider the phobic form of hypochondriac fixations summarized below (which the *DSM-IV* places with problems of psychosomatic origin) as a disorder based on fear because we have observed, in these disorders, a perceptive and reactive dynamic of a phobic-obsessive type.

Hypochondria: Diagnostic Criteria

a. The fear of having a serious disease based on the (garbled) interpretation of bodily signals or sensations. No diagnostic evidence of real physical problems. Average age at appearance, 20 to 30 years. Generally chronic development, with disappearances and reappearances of the symptom. However, many cases recover. Predispositions: it seems to be frequent in persons who have had or whose family members have had health problems. Psychosocial stress factors also seem to influence this disorder.
b. Appropriate diagnoses do not show organic diseases, but patients do not believe this and continue with their own interpretations. The symptom is not a panic attack.
c. The fear of being seriously ill continues even after medical reassurance.
d. The symptom lasts for at least six months.

Chapter 2 describes how the perceptive-reactive systems of all these typologies of fear-related problems function according to our model. Chapter 3 presents the specific forms of treatment we have devised for these typologies of problems. We shall now proceed to show how our study of these forms of phobic pathology followed rigorous methodology and how it was applied to a great number of subjects.

THE SUBJECTS OF OUR RESEARCH-INTERVENTION

The described typologies of disorders were treated in 152 patients in Italy. Our sample was unhampered by geographic, or possibly cultural, limitations, because within Italy there are many diverse subcultures and traditions.

Patients came for treatment on their own initiative. We have classified them by specific typologies of disorder for the purpose of this study.

The variables that these 152 patients have in common are the following:

1. having requested therapy at our center and having been treated according to our model of brief strategic therapy;

2. belonging, from a diagnostic point of view, to one of the typologies of phobic disorder described above;
3. having gone through a follow-up three months, six months and one year after their treatment was ended.

While 169 patients came to us for treatment, 17 abandoned the treatment within the first two sessions. Any considerations that might be made about this early abandonment of the treatment would seem unreliable.

There are 84 women and 68 men in our subject group. Their average age is 28 years; the youngest is 13 and the eldest 71. Diagnostically, there are 28 cases of agoraphobia (18 percent), 61 cases of panic attack with agoraphobia (40 percent), 14 cases of panic attack without agoraphobia (9 percent), 31 cases of phobic-obsessive compulsion (20 percent), and 18 cases of hypochondriac fixation (12 percent).

The results of our treatment of these severe forms of phobic problems through the brief-strategic model of therapy are presented in Chapters 3 and 4. The modalities of this treatment and the data that show the remarkable efficacy (ability to produce effective solutions to the problem) and good cost/benefit ratio of this therapeutic intervention are also presented. Chapter 4 presents the results that emerged from our research-intervention.

The Formation and Persistence
of Phobic Disorders

*Those who keep on asking "why" are like tourists who read the guidebook
while they are standing in front of a monument: they are so busy reading
about the monument's history, origins, etc., etc., that they don't even take
the time to look at it.*

Ludwig Wittgenstein

EPISTEMOLOGICAL CONSIDERATIONS

When discussing a psychological problem, it seems natural to ask what
caused it. There is, at the root of this question, a century-old conception
of the causality of things that assumes there is always a linear relationship
of cause and effect between natural events, both biological and physical.
From the perspective of linear causality, to solve a problem one must find
its initial causes. The causes come before the effects; thus, to resolve a problem in the present, an analysis of the past is considered necessary.

In our field, this reductive and obsolete concept of causality lies at
the root of traditional models of interpretation of mind and behavior. These

$$A \longrightarrow B \longrightarrow C \longrightarrow D$$

FIGURE 2–1. Linear causality.

models, some of which are antithetical to each other (for example, psychoanalysis and behaviorism), founded their theories and consequently their therapeutic interventions on a deterministic relationship between the causes and effects of events. Whether it is the "original trauma" of psychoanalysis or the "operating conditioning" of behaviorism makes little difference at the epistemological level.

This kind of epistemological model became obsolete more than a century ago in physics and the natural sciences. It is enough to think of Einstein's principle of relativity or Heisenberg's principle of indetermination, or the more recent studies by the biologists Maturana and Varela on the "autopoiesis" of living systems and the "dissipative structures" of the physicist Prigogine, to have a few examples of how contemporary science has distanced itself from an epistemology founded on conceptions of linear change, and adopted a concept of circular causality; that is, unidirectionality and linear causality, which can be expressed as in Figure 2–1, is abandoned in favor of a nondeterministic conception that is in harmony with contemporary epistemological theories of circular causality (Figure 2–2). Here the process assumes a circular form of reverberation through the reciprocal retroactions of its variables.

> Once such a circular process has been established, one can no longer talk about origins and results, causes and effects. The system must be studied in its totality, for the whole is more than, and different from, the mere sum of its parts. Any attempt to study the components in isolation would destroy the totality and would produce results that are of no help for our understanding of the system. Rather, the opposite is now the case: our understanding of any one component or function of the system presupposes our understanding of the system as a whole. [Nardone and Watzlawick 1993, p. 37]

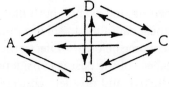

FIGURE 2–2. Circular causality.

This new epistemology entered the field of clinical psychology only a few decades ago, thanks to the work of the scholars of the Palo Alto school (Bateson, Watzlawick, Weakland, et al.). When they applied this innovative epistemological perspective to the clinical field, they produced a Copernican revolution in the psychological and psychiatric disciplines. Unfortunately, it takes much more than a few decades for scientific innovations to become known by the large public and integrated into the popular culture.

When trying to give explanations to patients who are looking for the causes of their phobias, we must first tell them that knowing the causes of a disturbance is neither necessary nor useful to its solution. In the task of changing a phobic-obsessive situation and steering it toward a complete extinction of the disorder, it does not help to know the causes of the problem or how it has developed over time. But it helps to study how this system of perception and reaction toward reality functions in the patient's here and now, or what we define as the patient's "perceptive-reactive system." As we shall see in Chapter 3, we devise and apply strategies that can change the workings of this dysfunctional system of perception and reaction toward reality, so as to lead the patient to a rapid and effective resolution of the problem.

Even when it has been proven that research into past causes is not useful in solving the present problem, a reader who is fascinated by journeys within the human soul would still maintain that unveiling the causes of the disturbance represents a pure intellectual pleasure, which, in any case, makes it an important pastime. Even so, unfortunately, this person would still fall into a series of inherent traps in the communication between the patient and the self and between the patient and others (in this case, the therapist). The final result would be a "construction" of the presumed causes on the basis of the adopted theories of reference. In other words, if their intention is to find the causes of the present problem, they will proceed by analyzing the patient's descriptions based on memories of his past life and the appearance of his problems. We have, in the patient's description, a first "translation" of reality, mediated by the ideas he holds in the present; if only for this reason, it will not be very reliable.

Moreover, there will be a second "translation," that of the therapist who interprets and explains the causes of the present psychological problem in light of his theories of reference. Clearly, these interpretative and communicative passages distort the "original reality," constructing an interpretation that is a "new reality," a product of the interaction between patient and therapist.

Finally, even if we could completely isolate facts from interpretations and theories, when trying to determine why a problem has established itself and formulating a causal explicative theory we would run into a problem raised by modern constructivist epistemology (Foerster 1973, Glaserfeld 1984, Watzlawick 1984) with respect to theories that explain everything, so-called self-sealing theories.[1] This problem is expressed in terms of the uniqueness and nonrepeatability of each single human personality (or better, human system) in its particular relationships with itself, others, and the world.

If we took similar events experienced by several persons as possible linear causes of the presenting problem, we would forget that every reality changes according to the perspective from which we perceive and elaborate it. The same event, experienced by persons who have different ways of relating to themselves, others, and the world, leads to radically different experiences that cannot, therefore, be generalized as causes of the problem. From that point of view, at the level of causal explicative theory, we assume the so-called single-case theory, in other words, the point of view that favors a specific theory for each specific case.

From our perspective, all these problems arise from the epistemologically incorrect search for the cause of a problem. In other words, as Wittgenstein would say, we too often consider whether our answers are right or wrong without considering whether the questions we ask are correct. From the perspective of studying a problem in search of its solutions, the important thing is to go from the question "Why does it exist?" to the question "How does it work?" We go from analyzing contents to analyzing processes; from a semantic analysis of the problem to a pragmatic evaluation of its functioning; from a physicalist and deterministic epistemological model to a cybernetic and constructivist one (Ashby 1954, 1956, Bateson 1967, 1972, 1979, Keeney 1985, Watzlawick 1984, Watzlawick et al. 1967, Weakland et al. 1974, Wiener 1947, 1967, 1975), and from a concept of rigid linearity between cause and effect to a concept of interaction—within problematic situations and between the persistence and the solution of problems (Watzlawick et al. 1974).

Assuming this alternative methodological perspective, we observe the functioning of the specific human system under analysis through interven-

---

1. Theoretical models that appear to be unfalsifiable in that they include and explain all events, and which therefore cannot be considered scientific.

tions aimed at changing this functioning. Having produced the change and solved the problem of fear, panic, and phobia in a considerable number of patients by applying structurally isomorphic procedure, we can say that, in our case, we have gained a knowledge of the workings, at the level of processes and dynamics, of human systems that function under a phobic perception of and reaction to reality.

We believe that it is possible to formulate a theory not of the "why" of fear, but rather of the "how" of the typical perceptive-reactive processes and dynamics of persons affected by phobic disorders function; in other words, not an explicative (causal) theory of fear but a cybernetic one. Our information concerns the persistence much more directly than the formation of the problem, for the reason that our knowledge of the phobic perceptive-reactive systems has been gained through strategic interventions that have ruptured the persistence of this system of perceiving and reacting to reality (i.e., the perverse game of retroactions that maintains the equilibrium of a phobic system). We believe, therefore, that our most important contribution in this chapter is our refusing to dwell on the origin of the problems under discussion.

Our alternative object of proposal is a hypothesis about how phobic disorders seem to start, focusing on a detailed exposition of how they persist and tend to grow worse. If our pragmatic aim is to change and resolve such problems, the only type of knowledge that is really useful is a knowledge of how such problems persist and are complicated by a network of perceptive and reactive retroactions between the subject and his personal and interpersonal reality.

FORMATION AND PERSISTENCE: AN EMPIRICAL STUDY

> The orthodoxy of reason contributes more than any religion to human foolishness.
>
> Karl Kraus

Some common convictions on how fears are formed and persist are strongly disconfirmed by the results of our research-intervention. The first to be invalidated is the hypothesis that severe forms of fear, like all psychological and behavioral disorders, have their origin in unresolved childhood traumas. On the contrary, so-called childhood traumas were reported in only three of our 152 cases. However, since those three cases had all undergone years of psychoanalytic treatment, we cannot know whether the trauma really had such great importance for the patients or whether the importance attributed to it was not the fruit of the psychoanalysts' interpretations and theories. These interpretations and the patients' successive *insights* had not led to any concrete therapeutic result.

The second hypothesis to be clearly disproven by our case study is that severe phobic disorders have a purely biological origin. Very fashionable a few decades ago, this theory has returned to the limelight in the past few years; this may be due to the commercial interests of pharmaceutical companies rather than to any concrete results in clinical and applied research. This theory states that panic attacks are provoked by a dysfunction of a part of the brain called the locus ceruleus, while obsessive-compulsive disorders arise from an insufficiency of serotonin, a neurotransmitter.

From an epistemological point of view, the claim to explain the functioning of such a complex system as the mind in terms of one single component seems decidedly reductive. As Birdwhistel puts it (1970), this is like trying to understand the entire New York sewer system by studying a five-inch section of it. Moreover, we must remember that the limits of each observation unit are always drawn by the observer.

If the purely biological hypotheses were realistic, then specific pharmaceutical interventions would produce complete recoveries. When such therapies produce no effects, or only partial effects, we have to doubt their validity. Of the 152 patients of our study-intervention, 131 (86 percent) had previously tried pharmacological treatment at centers specializing in the therapy of panic attacks; in 83 cases, after slight relief at the beginning, the pathology had remained unchanged; in 8 cases, it had worsened; and in 40 cases it had improved in that the phobic reactions (panic attacks) decreased, but since the patients' phobic perceptions had not changed, they continued to avoid situations perceived as fearsome.

These data clearly show that purely biological hypotheses on the origin and persistence of phobic disorders are invalid. In saying this, we do not wish to deny the presence of biological alterations in subjects affected by phobic-obsessive disturbances, nor, therefore, the frequent usefulness of parallel pharmacological or psychological therapies. We are stating only that a strictly reductivist biological view does not hold in the face of concrete evidence. In fact, 51 patients who showed positive results in our therapy were treated in collaboration with a specialist in pharmacological treatments. But the pharmacological therapies were gradually reduced to zero as the psychological therapy proceeded.

The third conviction to be decidedly disproven by our data concerns the presumed psychological fragility of subjects suffering from severe forms of fear, or their coming from hyperprotective or emotionally depriving families. In 91 of our cases (60 percent), the patient and their families told us that the patient had always been independent, quite courageous, and capable of facing all kinds of situations, until the day when the disorder prevented him or her from doing so. Markedly protective family situations with a relational climate of continuous disqualification of the subject's independence and personal capability were found in only 32 cases (21 percent). In only 11 cases (7 percent) did we find a conflictual family situation with a relational climate of emotional deprivation or disqualification. Even an evolutionary-cognitive and/or relational hypothesis on the origins of phobic disorders does not, therefore, appear to be valid in the light of our concrete data.

The fourth conviction to be denied by the detailed accounts of all 152 patients is that of a reflexological-mechanistic origin. This theory maintains that there is necessarily a linear causal relationship between an experience of frightening stimuli and the establishment of phobic responses. Most of our patients—103 (68 percent)—reported that they had had no experience of strong fear in connection with a concrete stimulus such as, for example, a fearsome event from which the phobic symptoms had originated. Moreover, even for the 49 patients (32 percent) who reported an initial upsetting event, this event seems not to have been directly determined by a concrete fact but, as we shall see, by a sort of progressive self-suggested building up of tension that led to the construction of the first attack of indomitable fear. On the basis of this episode, retroactive sequences leading to generalized phobic perception and reactions were established between the subject and realities.

If we analyze the process and the typical retroactions reported in relation to the emergence and formation of the disorder, that is, the accounts of how the problems appeared and evolved, we find isomorphic dynamics in almost every case. The severe phobic disorders appeared and gradually became more complicated on the basis of doubts and thoughts about the possibility of becoming ill. These doubts had started to flash through the patient's mind, either without any real motivation, or on the basis of a first slight episode of motivated fear of illness.

In the first group of patients (103 cases, 68 percent) the thoughts were of the following kind: "I might feel ill in a crowd of people, or far away from home." "Who will help me?" and "What a sorry appearance I will make." Gradually, these doubts became true phobic fixations on the basis of which the patients began to activate the typical behavior of avoidance and escape from what they thought might unleash such a chain of thoughts and emotions. The patients are afraid of all the physical reactions (tachycardia, breathing difficulties, vertigo, sweating, confusion) that such emotional situations repeatedly set in motion.

In the second group of patients (49 cases, 32 percent) the same process was activated when, on the basis of a first episode of fear and somatic symptoms, the patients entered into a state of permanent alert against their own reactions. Having noticed that some situations created strong emotional reactions (and consequent somatic symptoms), they also activated the behavior of avoidance and escape, or attempted to control their physical reactions—all of which had the result of complicating and aggravating the symptoms.

As these observations show, severe forms of phobic disorder are initiated by events that are not particularly severe from a physical point of view, or even by purely mental events such as the doubt: "I might feel sick." It seems that these patients fall into the same mental trap as the centipede that began to think about how difficult it was to move all its hundred feet at the same time, and consequently started to want to control and direct that spontaneous ability, with the result that he could no longer walk.

In fact, as we shall see more extensively later on, it seems that what determines the establishment of a strong phobic symptomatology is not the initial event but all that the phobic person does to avoid fear. The attempted solutions applied in order to escape the fear that one's own frightening emotional and somatic reactions will be unleashed lead to the aggravation of the symptomatology and end up stabilizing the symptoms at a higher level of severity, that of a complete generalization of the phobic perceptions of and reactions to reality. At this point, the person has reached what has been defined as *helplessness*.

> "Learned helplessness," i.e., learned impotence, has been studied by cognitive psychotherapists who have identified it with the condition of not being able to control events. When facing such an experience, the individual ends up expecting to be unable to exert any influence on future ones. The greatest probability of developing a strong emotional disorder occurs if the cause is perceived as more "internal," i.e., deriving from personal incapacity, than "external." The condition of learned helplessness can determine three psychological conditions: depression;

a reaction of acute and chronic fear of a persecutory kind; the recourse to rituals and beliefs that may control the menace of feared events. Cognitive mediations, personality variables, and, above all, culturally available response patterns all influence what type of defensive action there will be. [Salvini 1991, p. 14]

To clarify the construct that the persistence of a problem is maintained by the solutions applied in attempts to resolve that problem, we can look at a concrete example. A person who is afraid of feeling ill, afraid of leaving home, usually applies two basic attempted solutions. The first is to avoid leaving the house alone and shunning all situations that might entail the risk of having to be alone away from home, and sometimes even at home. Understandably, this behavior gradually leads to the avoidance of almost everything. But this form of generalized avoidance also lowers the subject's threshold of fear activation, so that the subject's efforts to control the fearsome situations by avoiding them, leads to a vertiginous increase of such situations, to the point that even minimal distances or moments of solitude will precipitate a panic attack. Thus, the attempted solution retroacts on the problem and complicates it.

The second attempted solution usually applied by persons who suffer from severe forms of fear is to ask for help. They constantly request massive support from the people around them, and sometimes show true signs of genius in their building up around themselves a support network of people who are ready to intervene in case there should be an attack of fear. But even this laborious protective solution, which redundantly confirms the subject's state of presumed "illness" at the level of interpersonal communication, will gradually contribute to the maintenance and aggravation of the symptoms. Every time the patient requests and receives help, he or she receives a double message: (1) "I help you and protect you because I love you"; (2) "I help and protect you because you are ill." The redundant repetition of this message increasingly confirms the severity of the illness to the patient and, functioning as a self-fulfilling prophecy, it tends to aggravate the symptoms. In this case also, the attempted solution retroacts on the problem and complicates it instead of resolving it.

These two attempted solutions form a recursive sequence of behavior and experience within which what ought to free the patient from fear maintains it instead. Researchers in cybernetics have shown how situations are kept stable because of recursive processes of retroactions between the contributing factors. As Keeney (1985) notes, according to this descriptive criterion, agoraphobic patients can be defined as individuals who are prisoners of a faulty recursive sequence that also includes the behavior by which they attempt to resolve the problem. In this kind of process, every attempt to avoid open spaces only perpetuates other escapes from open spaces. The attempts to overcome the problem contribute to determining the problem and maintaining it.

It seems, therefore, that the interaction between the subject and his fear becomes a proper cybernetic system with a specific recursive organization of behavior and a structure founded on retroactions that maintain its stability and balance. In this case, the balance is dysfunctional or pathological for the subject.

Once such a process has been set in motion (often accidentally, as in most of our cases) and a dynamic of circular retroaction between subject and reality has established itself on the basis of a perception of fear, the dynamic will tend to remain constant. This retroactive dynamic is kept constant by the subject's very efforts to work toward change; an intervention by someone who is external to the cybernetic system is, therefore, absolutely necessary if an actual change is to be produced.

From that perspective, therefore, severe phobic disorders do not appear to be the result of a specific and certain cause; instead, they are the result of a complex process of retroactions between the subject and reality, a process set in motion by an event that often has no connection with the typology of disorder that later develops.

In other words, what starts the process that leads to the formation of what we define as the phobic perceptive-reactive system is not an event that results from a certain and controllable causality, but a kind of accidental fluctuation that leads to the first direct, or only imaginary, experience of fear. From that first casual event, a severe phobic symptomatology is established by a gradual but disruptive chain reaction based on the retroaction between the subject and reality.

Severe phobic disorders thus appear to be set in motion by the "butterfly effect" of Thom's (1990) theory of catastrophes: the flutter of a butterfly's wings in Africa can, if it happens at a certain moment in space and time, start a chain of natural retroactions that will lead to a hurricane in the Caribbean. In our specific case, the butterfly effect is represented by that first accidental, real or imaginary experience that introduces a new perceptive-reactive possibility within the subject's mind: the possibility of fear. All that the subject later does in defense against this new terrifying perception of reality, if such actions do not properly reframe the perceptive-reactive system but merely serve as a temporary support, will only provide further reinforcements of this perception and aggravate its effects by generalizing the fear and increasing the related psychological and behavioral responses.

At that point, the person becomes imprisoned within a system of perception of reality that is founded on fear; and this inevitably leads to strongly symptomatic behavioral reactions.

The most important aspect from the clinical perspective on intervention thus seems to be that the formation and (even more so) the persistence of severe phobic-obsessive symptomatologies are not determined by original causes, but by attempted solutions applied by the patient as a self-defense against fear. These dysfunctional attempted solutions gradually establish and maintain the rigidity of the patient's perceptive-reactive system.

According to this analysis, severe forms of phobic disorder appear as a recursive self-reverberating system, a system that is decidedly similar to the autopoiesis of natural systems described by Maturana and Varela. Practically, once it has formed, this type of autopoietic system no longer needs real external stimuli to have certain defined recursive reactions, since it "constructs" a phobic perceptive-reactive system within itself. A patient who has formed such an autopoietic system does not strictly need concrete situations of fear to have phobic reactions, because the patient is, by her own mental processes, "constructing" such realities, which she, however, perceives as originating from a tangible external reality.

Once established, the recursive system of retroaction between the subject and reality tends to maintain itself; in other words, the balance of the system persists even though it is dysfunctional, and even though, seen from the outside, it may look like an imbalance. To be broken, this type of persistence requires interventions that change not only the patients' behavioral reactions but also their cognitive organization and, above all, their perceptions of reality. Otherwise, the change will be only temporary and the balance based on the network of retroactions of the phobic perception will rapidly reestablish itself in an adaptive response by the organism to a reality that has been produced by the same organism.

To make this clearer and more explicit, we believe it is necessary to explain how such a process is established in the specific forms of phobic disorder by giving some examples. In the different typologies of severe phobic disorders cited in Chapter 1, we have observed isomorphic perceptive-reactive mechanisms; these, however, structure some variants on the basic theme of interaction between the persistence of the problem and the attempted solutions.

ATTEMPTED SOLUTIONS AND PERSISTENCE OF THE AGORAPHOBIC PERCEPTIVE-REACTIVE SYSTEM

The greatest of strengths is unequal to the energy that some people employ to defend their own weakness.

Karl Kraus

Patients with this type of problem report a first, real or imaginary, experience of feeling uneasy or anxious with the appearance of somatic symptoms, in contexts where the patient felt alone, incapable, and impotent about these feelings.

Following that episode, the patient put two attempted solutions into effect: (1) avoidance; (2) seeking help from family and friends.

These two dysfunctional attempted solutions gradually construct a personal situation where the patient becomes incapable of exploration, or incapable of leaving his "safe place"; the patient also becomes totally unable to do anything whatsoever without the company of another person.

The first avoidance leads to a chain of avoidances, until the patient starts to avoid all personal exposure. Partly thanks to the relational retro-actions from the people who propose themselves as protectors, the patient's request for help and social support gradually makes this help and support become absolutely necessary in any situation of exploration or leaving home. When this system has repeated itself for a long time, it becomes a spontaneous, self-supporting, and self-feeding psychic and behavioral organization.

Rationally, by logical analysis, the patient knows that his perceptions and actions are dysfunctional, but he cannot act differently. As rigid as granite, that perceptive-reactive system toward reality has become established, and forces feelings and actions upon the subject that he is unable to change or control.

As we shall see in the next chapter, our therapeutic intervention on the two attempted solutions described above breaks their recursiveness;

thus, it also breaks the recursiveness and persistence of the agoraphobic patient's entire perceptive-reactive system. From a cybernetic point of view, such interactive mechanisms are the homeostasis of that specific dysfunctional balance; from a pragmatic point of view, they are the two levers on which we can put strategic pressure in order to get a change going.

ATTEMPTED SOLUTIONS AND PERSISTENCE OF THE PANIC ATTACK SYNDROME

In this typology of phobic disorder, we observe an initial real or imaginary episode of strong anxious somatic symptoms (tachycardia, fainting, a feeling of great mental confusion, loss of balance, breathing difficulties, and so on), or a strong fear that one is going to be sick.

This first experience starts a reaction of attempted control of one's bodily functions, which results in an anxious blockage or malfunctioning of the same. Practically speaking, if a person begins to listen to his own heartbeat while worrying that it will become altered, the prophecy will punctually fulfill itself, and the cardiac rhythm will indeed be altered. The same is true for other spontaneous organic functions that are inhibited or altered when submitted to enforced rational control. Thus, the subject's attempt to control menacing organic alterations has the result of calling them forth. Here again, the attempted solution is feeding the problem.

In many cases of this typology of disorder, the patient starts wanting to control his fear of the disorder, thus obviously feeding it even more. This leads to the formation of a "fear of fear" that maintains and complicates the problem.

To this contorted network of paradoxical retroactions applied by the patient, we must add the social retroactions of attempted protection from his family and friends; these confirm to the subject the seriousness of his condition. And to that, we must add the reductivist (as we have explained above) psychiatric classification that defines panic attacks as a purely organic disease. This labeling function sustains, and sometimes aggravates, the problem; in Watzlawick's words, "The diagnosis constructs the pathology" (Zeig 1992, p. 55).

While the interaction between persistence and attempted solutions of the problem that has been observed in agoraphobic patients is based on avoidance and help seeking, in subjects with panic attacks this interaction, which feeds the symptom instead of reducing it, is based on an obsessive attempt, and need, to control the symptom. Requesting family support and medical intervention appears to be a necessity that the subject has conflicts about.

The first move in the strategic intervention concentrates on stopping the vicious circle of listening for, and attempting to control, physical and psychological reactions. This retroactive and recursive mechanism is both a homeostasis and a lever for changing the balance of the perceptive-reactive system of panic.

ATTEMPTED SOLUTIONS AND PERSISTENCE OF THE COMPOSITE AGORAPHOBIA AND PANIC ATTACK SYNDROME

In this type of disorder, we simultaneously find interactions between attempted solutions and persistence of the problems that belong to agoraphobia and to the panic attack syndrome. Sometimes the agoraphobic syndrome is complicated by panic attacks; in other cases, on the contrary, the panic attack syndrome is complicated by agoraphobic symptoms.

We have not found any usual temporal order of causality between these two kinds of disorder; it seems that each of them can be complicated by being joined by the other symptomatology.

We find here the attempted solutions of avoidance, help seeking, and obsessively controlling internal reactions. An attempted pharmacological solution is usually added. Thus, many elements contribute to maintaining the balance of this typology of a perceptive-reactive system. Therefore, to start a change, we need to intervene on all the different equilibrators of the system simultaneously.

However, our clinical experience has shown that some variation in our order of therapeutic moves is necessary, depending on which of the two perceptive-reactive systems is the prevailing one. If the person has developed an agoraphobic disorder based on a panic attack syndrome, the first lever on which to put pressure will be the attempted solution of obsessively controlling physical and mental reactions; later, we will intervene on the other attempted solutions that are maintaining the problem.

If, on the contrary, panic attacks have appeared on the basis of an agoraphobic perceptive-reactive system, our first objective will be to stop the vicious circle of avoidance and help seeking; then we proceed to disconnect the other attempted solutions that are maintaining the balance of the system.

ATTEMPTED SOLUTIONS AND PERSISTENCE OF THE OBSESSIVE-COMPULSIVE SYNDROME

In this typology of phobic disorder we have observed that, when seized by an uncontrolled or avoided fear, patients start to perform rituals believed to have the power of driving this indomitable fear away. (These disparate rituals range from the simple repetition of one action to extremely complicated sequences: decontaminating washings, endlessly repeated formulas and prayers, or other unusual behavior.)

The performance of a protective or propitiatory ritual gives the subject the momentary illusion of being able to control the fear, but for this same reason it also forces the subject to a more and more frequent obsessive repetition of the ritual. In many cases that we have treated, daily life had simply become a succession of rituals. In this pathology it is even more obvious that the attempted solution itself becomes the problem in obsessive-compulsive syndromes, once the interaction between persistence and attempted solution to the problem has started and established itself, the most urgent need felt by the patients is to be liberated from the slavery of this obligatory performance of rituals.

In this type of case, the attempted solution, or homeostasis of the dysfunctional balance of the symptomatology, seems to be an attempt to drive away the fear through the performance of protective rituals that in turn, performed obsessively, become the main symptom. For the patient, the rituals have the important function of contrasting the fear, but the fear increases as an effect of this contrast and forces the patient to increase the performances of rituals. The vicious circle of dysfunctional retroactions between the patient and reality, therefore, has the appearance of an autopoietic system. Having set in, the system becomes self-feeding, and paradoxically maintains its own persistence through the very efforts toward change.

In contrast to the perceptive-reactive systems analyzed above, the obsessive-compulsive system is sustained by the effort to fight fear by the attempted solution of protective or propitiatory rituals. But just like in the typologies described earlier, the "ritual battle" between attempted solutions and persistence simultaneously represents both the homeostasis and the entropy of the balance of the obsessive-compulsive system of perception and reaction.

ATTEMPTED SOLUTIONS AND PERSISTENCE OF THE PHOBIC-HYPOCHONDRIAC SYNDROME

We have observed that the first episode in this type of disorder is that the patient is afraid of having contracted a serious illness. This occurs, after a variable interval, after (1) a real illness experienced by the patient; (2) an illness that has affected someone dear to the patient; (3) the patient has read, heard on the radio, seen on television, or in other ways learned some news regarding the symptoms of some serious disease (cancer, heart disease, AIDS).

On the basis of this new information or experience that has entered the patient's mind, he or she begins to listen obsessively to oneself, searching for any possible physical signs of the presumed illness. In the case of panic attacks, for example, the prophecy is obviously self-fulfilling and the patient will perceive alarming signals in his or her body—undisputable signals of a serious illness. The reaction of controlling one's own body diagnostically produces the observation of signs of organic alterations, and this leads to an increase in the obsessive attention, which, in turn, increases perceptions of alterations in the organism. Here again we observe the setting in of a cybernetic system of self-feeding retroactions that is kept going by an interaction of reciprocal preservation between attempted solution and persistence of the problem.

In such cases, medical diagnoses denying the subject's persuasions and fears paradoxically increase these fears and fixations instead of reducing them. On receiving a negative diagnosis, the hypochondriac patient will think the diagnostic methods are not precise enough, and will therefore request even more sophisticated medical testing, or will believe that his or her illness is so obscure that no diagnosis can detect it. In this persuasion, the patient starts to apply the second attempted solution, an almost infinite process of diagnostic tests and the request of close to full-time medical assistance. All medical intervention, diagnostic or pharmacological, will be interpreted as confirming the patient's presumed illness, and will thus function as an additional attempted solution that complicates the problem instead of resolving it.

The phobic-hypochondriac obsessive-reactive system is similar to the panic attack system, with the difference that in cases of panic attack, the patients try to control and restrain the symptoms, while phobic-hypochondriac patients only try to detect the symptoms and then seek medical help. Here we find no efforts to control symptoms and no conflicts about asking for help, but an obsessive observation of physical signs that can justify a request for specialistic intervention. This state of expectancy of an illness is so stressful to the patient that real psychosomatic disturbances often appear.

This perceptive-reactive system thus maintains its state of dysfunctional equilibrium through the application of two attempted solutions: (1) obsessive attention devoted to listening to one's own body in a paradoxical search for signs of illness that punctually arrive; (2) an equally paradoxical quest through unendingly repeated medical diagnoses, for an answer that would prove scientifically that the patient is actually suffering from an obscure illness (it almost seems that these subjects would be happy if clinical diagnoses detected a real organic disease).

Our conclusion from a strategic point of view is that these interactive mechanisms simultaneously appear to be the homeostasis and the levers for changing the typical dysfunctional balance of phobic-hypochondriac syndromes.

A MODEL OF THE INTERACTION BETWEEN ATTEMPTED SOLUTIONS AND PERSISTENCE IN PHOBIC DISORDERS

Circumstances have less power than we think to make us happy or unhappy, but the anticipation of future circumstances in our imagination has an immense power.

Hugo von Hofmannsthal

After having described the different perceptive-reactive systems of the five phobic syndromes we have studied as an interaction between persistence and attempted change, it may be useful to summarize their cybernetic functioning and usual temporal sequence graphically (Figure 2–3):

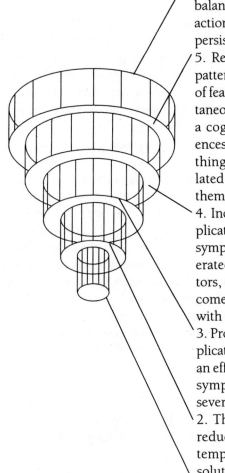

6. A system of perception and reaction toward reality, rigid in its dysfunctional balance (i.e., the vicious circle of interaction between attempted solution and persistence of the problem) sets in.

5. Redundant repetition, stiffening in patterns of reaction to and anticipation of fear, becomes an automatic and spontaneous mechanism no longer requiring a cognitive effort. The subject experiences the attempted solutions as something spontaneously and naturally related to fear, and is unable to control them.

4. Increasing attempted solutions complicate the problems even further. The symptomatology requires solutions operated by others (family, friends, doctors, etc.): the problem is starting to become part of broader systemic balances with related secondary effects.

3. Problems reach a higher level of complication: fear is momentarily reduced as an effect of the applied solutions, but the symptoms increase and become more severe.

2. The subject reacts with attempts to reduce, control, or fight fear (first attempted personal and interpersonal solutions).

1. A real or imagined initial event produces the first feeling of fear (first change of perspective toward reality.)

FIGURE 2–3. Cybernetic functioning and the temporal sequence. (The sequence starts at the bottom.)

As Salvini (1991) writes,

> Once the perverse game has set in, the significance attributed to real or imaginary menacing events is not only governed by culturally learned beliefs, but also by the way our mind works, that is, how our mind organizes the available information aside from content.
>
> Attributions of causality, categorizations of events, inferential and performative processes, our tendency to give a definitive meaning and a "narrative structure" to heterogeneous episodes and sequences of occurrences, and the application of prototypical and stereotypical schema all have important roles in organizing a (more or less justified) menacing interpretation of reality.
>
> At the level of content, "mental schema" also perform an evaluation of the facts, in the sense that they not only select and judge their relevance but also add missing elements and meanings, resolving any incongruities in such a way as to make them consistent with a theory on the reality at issue. [p. 15]

In other words, when the system of perception and reaction becomes rigid, the person will spontaneously organize any perception or information through the filter and the deforming lens of fear, and translate reality into the language of fear, thus transforming reality into something that is congruent and consistent with the person's rigid perceptive and cognitive organization.

At this point the reader, having observed that the patient's efforts to resolve the problem seem to determine its subsistence, might ask, "But what is it that makes people persist in behavior and actions that even they sometimes recognize as being dysfunctional to the solution of their problem? How is it that the agoraphobic person sticks to strategies of avoidance and help seeking despite the awareness that such actions are maintaining the problem? How is it that the obsessive-compulsive subject continues to perform rituals against frightening realities? How is it that a person who is obsessed by hypochondriac fears persists in the search of an illness that is denied by diagnoses?"

These questions seem perfectly legitimate; it is natural to suppose that conscious and reasonable beings, if informed and aware of certain dynamics, ought to be able to manage them in the direction of well-being. These questions can be answered by a few crucial arguments.

The first is that people often have obsolete psychological and medical concepts in mind, and find it difficult to understand or accept alternative ones. But this is a minimal and reductive argument that, in my opinion, is valid for only a few cases. What holds for the majority of cases is the constructivist rule that being conscious and aware of something does not mean being able to apply it. As Foerster would say, "The opposite is true," that is, "If you desire to see (and know), learn how to act" (Watzlawick 1984, p. 5). More often even people of high intellect and culture, who are capable of understanding the complexity of certain recursive, autopoietic, and paradoxical mechanisms, will understand but not be able to act any differently. By now the idea that we go from thought to action in change processes seems obsolete on the basis of concrete experiences of intervention. As we shall see, effective change not only involves changing cognition, but also changing the perceptions that excite emotions, which in turn influence cognition and behavior. To be effective, such a change in the perceptive-reactive perspective must occur through concrete experiences.

A second argument—undoubtedly a strong one—useful for understanding how the persistence described above functions at the level of repetition of the dysfunctional strategy, is related to the fact that the primary effects of solutions attempted by phobic patients are a temporary reduction of the symptom, an illusion of safety from fear, a feeling of being protected. This means that when a panic attack appears, the patient instinctively performs actions that will provide relief as quickly as possible. At that moment, the patient does not think about long-term effects, is not planning strategies, but only starting reactions based on momentary perceptions.

The attempted solutions, which we have shown to be the real homeostasis and complicators of the problem, function primarily as a method of momentary escape from fear. This is the reason for their initial strength and persistence.

Henry Laborit (1982), one of the greatest living biologists, describes the escape mechanism as follows:

> Through the cortex, we reach anticipation thanks to the memorized experience of gratifying or nociceptive acts, and elaborate a strategy to satisfy or avoid such acts. The organization of action occurs at three levels. The first, more primitive level, organizes action automatically without adaptive capacities by internal and/or external stimulation. The second level organizes action by taking previous experience into consideration thanks to one's memory of the agreeable or disagreeable, useful or noxious quality of the feeling that derived from that experience. The third level is that of desire. It is tied to the imaginary construct that anticipates the result of the action and the strategy to use so as to ensure the gratifying action, or the action that avoids the noci-

ceptive stimulus. The first level only has recourse to a present procedure, the second adds past experience to the present action, and the third responds to the present thanks to the experience of the past, and anticipating the future result. [pp. 19–20]

According to Laborit's brilliant exemplification of the organization of actions, and our direct clinical experience, it seems that after a patient has elaborated a sequence of actions (such as the one described in Laborit's schema) that have alleviated panic, or provided a feeling of relief from fear, the patient will tend to repeat that sequence.

The redundant repetition of such a fixed schema of retroactions establishes a rigidity of actions and retroactions, a sort of automatic organization of actions, like the first level described by Laborit. In other words, what begins as a learned modality to escape from fear, and is then confirmed and reinforced by experiences and through social relationships, becomes a spontaneous and uncontrolled reaction—a system of perception and reaction toward reality that is stiff and unyielding to reason.

The answer to the questions asked at the beginning of this section is that, when first applied, the attempted solutions seemed decidedly useful and functional to the patients who applied them. Patients repeat such attempted solutions, despite their being dysfunctional, on the basis of their previous functionality and because in moments of crisis they represent the sole available repertoire of responses that can alleviate the fear.

To break the rigid dysfunctional balance of our patients' typical perceptive-reactive systems, an intervention that aims to resolve the complicated problems described here must possess particular characteristics that will enable us to lead patients to change their ways of perceiving reality and consequently their ways of reacting to it.

The characteristics of such an intervention must be (1) an ability to change the vicious circle of homeostatic retroactions between the persistence and the attempted solutions to the problem; (2) an ability to overcome the resistances to change that are typical of any system (and even stronger in complex ones, such as human systems), making the system change without the patient noticing it; (3) an ability to produce concrete experiences of change in perception and reaction toward the feared reality; (4) after the change, the ability to make the patients capable of recovering their emotional and behavioral resources and self-esteem.

With these objectives in mind, we have prepared a specific model of therapy that makes it possible to solve severe phobic disorders quickly and effectively.

3

Change and Solution

The strongest proof against any theory is its application.

Karl Kraus

EPISTEMOLOGICAL PREMISES, HYPOTHESES, AND INITIAL EXPERIMENTS IN PREPARING THE TREATMENT

We have found the persistence of severe forms of panic and phobia to be a complex organization of retroactions between the subject and reality. The functioning of this organization is maintained by the subject's dysfunctional system of perceptions and attempted solutions.

This complex interactive system includes the subject's relationship with self, others, and the world; it is paradoxically kept alive by the individual's efforts to change and by the efforts of other people who are drawn into this complex cybernetic network of retroactions.

As we shall see, changing this rigid and complex situation is a difficult but not impossible task. Its difficulty lies in the fact that, to obtain an effective resolution of the problems in a short time, we must lead the patients to change their reactions and, more than that, their perceptions. But to do that, we must also change our patients' ways of organizing the information they perceive, because the elaboration of data can markedly influence information.

Our experience with the large sample described in the previous chapters has shown that to obtain a second-order change,[1] in other words, a true leap in the quality and logical level of the interaction between the patient and reality, our intervention must simultaneously change the patients' reactive-behavioral modes (subjective attempted solutions), their ways of perceiving and elaborating data, and their social interactions (solutions attempted by others). To produce these changes, our interventions must create tangible experiences of different ways of perceiving, and reacting to, frightening realities, and also help the patients to change their cognitive elaboration of those experiences.

In working toward these ends, our most difficult task lies in overcoming the phobic perceptive-reactive system's resistance to change. Our interventions are, therefore, organized into strategies that employ suggestions, paradoxes, and "kind tricks" that force patients to adopt alternative ways of perceiving and reacting, and lead them to consequent cognitive and relational changes in the wake of concrete experiences under the guidance of the therapist. To lead patients through concrete experiences of change in their perceptive-reactive modalities, the therapist must start by making them do something without realizing it; otherwise, fear and resistance to change would prevent them from having the experiences that are indispensable to change.

That is why we believe it necessary to utilize suggestion techniques, paradoxes, and communicative and behavioral traps to reach the patient's

---

1. A second-order change is thus defined by Watzlawick and colleagues (1974):

> There are two types of change: one that occurs within a given system which itself remains unchanged, and one whose occurrence changes the system itself. To exemplify this distinction in more behavioral terms, a person having a nightmare can do many things in his dream—run, hide, fight, scream, jump off a cliff—but no change from any of these behaviors within the world of the dream would ever terminate the nightmare. *We shall henceforth refer to this kind of change as first-order change.* The one way out of the nightmare involves a change from dreaming to waking. Waking, obviously, is no longer part of the dream, but a change to an altogether different state. *This kind of change will from now on be referred to as second-order change.* [p. 27]

and therapist's common aim—a quick and effective solution of the presented problem.

Milton Erickson, Jay Haley, John Weakland, and Paul Watzlawick are the masters of this art of injunction—direct, indirect, or paradoxical reframing and behavioral prescriptions that can lead subjects through concrete experiences and toward quick and effective resolutions of their problems.

Therapy, in this perspective, becomes a sort of duel between the therapist and the patient; to reach the final victory, the therapist must find a way around the resistance to change that is typical of the patient's perceptive-reactive system. But let us emphasize, once again, that in this duel the therapist's victory is also the patient's, just as a defeat would also be shared by both. Therefore, if manipulative techniques can speed up the intervention and make it more efficacious, it seems perfectly legitimate that the therapist should have recourse to them.

Before describing our model of intervention in detail, we should mention that various types of intervention were tested in the preparatory stages of devising our technique, but were later discarded because they had either proved to be inefficacious or too costly in terms of the time necessary to obtain results.

A brief account of our experimental work on these techniques will help us justify to the reader how we came to prepare and sometimes invent strategies, setting up a treatment protocol by which quick and effective solutions can be produced.

We selected a series of therapeutic techniques from the existing literature on the treatment of phobic disorders and tested these techniques by direct application.

The first strategies to be adopted were derived from the behaviorist tradition of modification of phobic behavior (Bandura 1974, 1977, Skinner 1938, 1974, Wolpe 1958, 1973). We found that this typology of intervention was efficacious when applied to simpler forms of phobia (so-called monophobias[2]), but inefficacious against severe and generalized forms of fear.

---

2. Phobias against one specific object, or situation, or animal, for example, a fear of dogs, a fear of water, stage fright, and so on. These forms of phobia are nongeneralized forms of disorder: the patients have not constructed a perceptive-reactive system toward reality that is based on fear; they only have phobic reactions in the presence of specific stimuli.

Specifically, the usual behaviorist procedures were observed to have the following effects: (1) systematic desensitization initially produced a reduction of anxiety symptoms, but symptomatic relapses ineluctably followed; (2) modeling and guided exploration with agoraphobic patients produced a slight reduction of the patients' fear of going out, but had no effect at all on their inability to do anything without social support.

In practice, we have observed that when we employ systematic desensitization, we work on a decrease in behavioral symptoms but without even minimally intervening on the perceptions and cognitive elaborations that lead to such behavior. After some initial improvement, therefore, the unchanged phobic perception of reality ineluctably leads the patient back to again presenting even the initial phobic behaviors.

"Modeling" and guided exploration with agoraphobics did not modify the attempted solution of seeking help and social support; on the contrary, these techniques provoked more requests for help and thus left the agoraphobic perceptive-reactive system basically unchanged.

We also tested relaxation and self-control techniques such as autogenic training and self-hypnosis (Goldwurm et al. 1986); these types of intervention had the following effects.

In patients with agoraphobia and obsessive compulsions without panic attacks, we observed a slight improvement in the general level of anxiety, but no change in the patients' perceptions of menacing external realities nor, consequently, any change in their reactions to these realities.

Relaxation techniques had a paradoxical effect on most phobic symptomatologies based on sudden panic attacks, in that teaching these patients to listen more to their internal physical and mental reactions led to an exacerbation of the panic symptomatology. That this should have been the effect seems very understandable today. We have learned that such strategies encourage the dysfunctional attempted solution of listening to and controlling oneself; this solution has been identified as a reverberator of the problem in patients with panic attacks, compulsions, and hypochondria.

To change the support structure and stop reinforcements of the "designated patient's" symptomatology in the patient's relationships with others, we tried intervening on phobic patients' family interactions. Interventions on family behavior produced two kinds of effects. First, after a few attempts, the family inevitably gave in to the emotional blackmail of the phobic patients' help seeking; second, the patients in therapy expressed strongly aggressive feelings toward the therapist for "trying to put my family against me."

In our opinion, the main limitation of this kind of intervention from the point of view of its specific effect on phobic disorders is that it focuses mainly on the relationship between the patient and others, neglecting the more fundamental type of relationship that underlies phobic disturbances, namely the relationship between the patient and self. This concept is based on what we might define as the "relational bias" of strict family therapies (Andolfi 1991, Boscolo et al. 1988, Selvini-Palazzoli et al. 1989), and leads to a type of intervention that does not in the least affect the fundamental and central dynamic between the phobic patient and reality, which is expressed in the need to avoid or control the panic attack. On the contrary, this type of intervention increments the patient's fear, by adding the fear that the therapist's prescriptions will cause a loss of support and help from others. The patient, therefore, rebels, and usually this rebellion—expressed in the family or within the patient's relationship with the therapist—leads to a failure of the therapy.

We also tried the cognitivist and cognitive-behavioral approach (Beck and Emery 1985, Guidano 1988, Lorenzini and Sassaroli 1987, Mahoney 1979, Reda 1986). Some of the techniques utilized by cognitivist therapists proved to be efficacious, but the usual therapeutic procedure based on behavioral changes as effects of a gradually increasing awareness and change in the disturbed patient's cognitive organization proved scarcely effective because it was too time-consuming (from one to two years of therapy).

From our point of view, the low efficiency of this approach is due to the fact that according to cognitivist therapists change is reached by the gradual modification in the organization of the disturbed patient's cognitive structures. To obtain this result, cognitive therapists proceed by a gradual reframing at the cognitive level of the mental organization.

These procedures do not sufficiently take into account the fact that every system of perceptive-reactive organization, which is a form of equilibrium even when it is pathological, resists change. If change is necessarily the product of a gradual growth process based on insight and consciousness, then resistance to change will become stronger. In our opinion, this explains the excessive treatment time of cognitive interventions. Most such interventions, however, have efficacious results.

These considerations have led us to the empirical observation that, if we want to produce quick and effective changes in phobic-obsessive disorders, we have to utilize techniques of suggestion that can quickly overcome the resistance to change put up by these rigid, dysfunctional human systems. However, we have chosen some techniques from the cognitive-behaviorist approach and adopted them in the present model of brief therapy.

Our experiments did not include any techniques from psychodynamic approaches because, according to the relevant literature, this approach is hardly efficacious and absolutely ineffective in dealing with severe forms of phobic disorders.

As already mentioned, the techniques of the present model have come mainly from the following therapeutic approaches: (1) Erickson's strategic approach, particularly his later work based on injunctions, reframing, and behavioral prescriptions with suggestive communication and personal influence but without formal induction of hypnotic trance; and (2) the brief systemic-strategic therapy of the Mental Research Institute (Watzlawick et al. 1974) for its rigorous synthesis between studies on human communication (Watzlawick 1984, Watzlawick et al. 1967), the tradition and experience of systemic therapy, and the contributions based on Erickson's work.

The strategic-constructivist approach to brief therapy (Nardone 1991, Nardone and Watzlawick 1993), of which the present model of brief therapy of phobic-obsessive disorders represents the best expression, is derived from a synthesis of these approaches, their adaptation to the Italian cultural context, and a selection of other therapeutic techniques (Bandler and Grinder 1975a, b, de Shazer 1982, 1985, 1991, 1994, Fisch et al. 1982b, Haley 1976, Watzlawick 1984, Watzlawick et al. 1974, Weakland et al. 1974).

Thus, as we shall see, we have developed a model of therapy that can quickly break down the dysfunctional rigidity of the patients' perceptive-reactive systems and lead the patients through a series of concrete experiences of change, to the extinction of their symptoms, and to a reframing and to a flexible reorganization of their perceptive, cognitive, and behavioral modalities.

THE BRIEF STRATEGIC MODEL OF THERAPY FOR PHOBIC DISORDERS

> We should not judge human beings by what they do not know, but by what they know, and how they know it.
>
> Luc de Chapiers de Vanvenargues

Before describing the specific therapeutic strategies for the different perceptive-reactive systems described in Chapter 2, it will be useful to present the order of succession of our model of therapy, schematically subdivided into four consecutive stages, each of which is composed of (1) specific goals, (2) specific techniques to be utilized to achieve these goals, and (3) the most suitable typology of communication for that specific stage of therapeutic interaction.

In this approach to the solution of human problems, we attempt to determine the following:

1. how actions are based on goals. The solution strategy is based on the goals to reach, and not on the therapist's previous normative theory;
2. how, to resolve a problem, we intervene not on hypothetical causes, but on the patient's attempted solutions that maintain the problem instead of resolving it;
3. how the intervention is always adapted to the problem by constructing a rigorous strategic plan;
4. how, in order to obtain results in a short time, this rigorous strategic plan provides that we initially use methods of suggestion that make it possible to find a way around resistances to change and to break the perceptive-reactive system that is maintaining the problem. Later we provide redefinitions of the first therapeutic change and the following ones, which have the aim of making the subject more and more aware of his own abilities and personal autonomy. To that end, we progressively diminish the utilization of suggestion until it disappears completely in the course of the "therapeutic evolution" (Nardone 1991, p. 62).

Summary of the Model of Treatment

First Stage: First Session

Objectives

1. Define the problem and suggestive capture the patient.
2. Agree on goals, build on the therapeutic relationship, establish trust and collaboration.
3. Investigate the patient's perceptive-reactive system and redefine it.
4. Construct a hypothesis for intervention.
5. Begin the opening moves.

Strategies

1. "Tracing" technique
2. Circular reframing of the problem
3. Circular reframing of the perceptive-reactive system and attempted solutions
4. Paradoxical reframing
5. Confusion technique
6. Injunctions through metaphor
7. Indirect prescriptions

Communication

Hypnotic language (hypnosis without trance, active listening, nonverbal suggestions, and personal influence) is used.

Second Stage: From the Second to the Fifth Session

Objectives

1. Break the rigid perceptive-reactive system and the attempted solutions.
2. Redefine the first change.
3. Stimulate further, progressive changes.
4. Change the patient's perception of reality.

Strategies

1. Reframings: (a) paradoxical, (b) provocative, (c) doubt
2. Behavioral prescriptions: (a) direct, (b) indirect, (c) paradoxical
3. Injunctions by metaphor: (a) anecdotes, (b) stories, (c) aphorisms
4. Cognitive-explicative redefinitions of the changes obtained

Communication

Hypnotic language (hypnosis without trance or injunctive language) and maximum personal influence are used.

Third Stage: From the Sixth Session Onward

Objectives

1. Direct experiences of overcoming the problem.
2. Further progressive changes until the objectives that were agreed to be the resolution of the problem have been reached.
3. Redefine perceptions and relationship with self, others, and the world.
4. Consolidate the obtained results.
5. Facilitate the patient's acquisition of a flexible perception of and reaction to reality.

Strategies

1. Direct or indirect behavioral prescriptions (given in a gradually less injunctive style)
2. Reframings
3. Paradoxical anticipations of relapse
4. Explicative redefinitions of the changes and incentives toward personal autonomy

Communication

The language utilized is less and less hypnotic. There is a progressively diminishing use of personal influence and injunction in order to indirectly favor personal autonomy.

Fourth Stage: From the Fifth to the Last Session

Objectives

Complete acquisition of personal autonomy and perceptive-reactive flexibility by the patient.

Strategies

1. Detailed explanation of the work done (cognitive redefinition) and elucidation of the process of change is given.

2. Responsibility for the change is attributed to the patient and his personal resources.

Communication

Not hypnotic, but descriptive and colloquial (indicative language[3]) is used.

We now show how our model is applied specifically to each form of severe disorder based on fear. We shall present some concrete examples of brief-strategic interventions on phobic disorders to show, step by step, how the perceptive-reactive systems of each specific form of phobic disorder described in Chapter 2 has been reorganized in such a way as to free the patients of the disorder and to enable them to face their existential reality autonomously and with personal competence.

STRATEGY AND STRATAGEMS FOR THE SOLUTION OF AGORAPHOBIA

The particular is subordinated to the general, but the general must adapt itself to the particular.

Goethe

To break the rigidity of the agoraphobic perceptive-reactive system quickly, we apply a series of tactical moves within a general strategy.

At the beginning, we essentially focus on how to break the vicious circle of attempted solutions usually applied by agoraphobic subjects (avoidance and help seeking).

The techniques utilized to stop these two attempted solutions in the first stage of treatment are an indirect prescription (of the log notes) based on the hypnotic procedure of shifting the patient's attention away from the symptom, and a strategic reframing (fear of help) that utilizes the strength of the symptom against itself, using fear to provoke a change in the behavior that had been induced by the fear itself.

---

3. This model of therapeutic intervention is discussed and analyzed in detail elsewhere (Nardone 1991, Nardone and Watzlawick 1993).

In the ancient oriental art of fighting by stratagems (Anonymous 1991), these two well-known tactical maneuvers are called "ploughing the ocean, unknown to the sky"—calling attention upon some curious but unimportant action while carrying out an inconspicuous but crucial one; and "putting out the fire by letting the water boil over"—sending the adversary's own weight and strength back against him.

After these first two important maneuvers, we finally break the rigidity and self-referentiality of the perceptive-reactive system by the injunction of a paradoxical ritual. We prescribe that the symptom be deliberately exasperated within a preestablished ritual sequence, punctuated in time and space by the performance of actions prescribed under suggestion. By prescribing the symptom, this strategy paradoxically leads the patient to gain control over the symptom, or to make it disappear completely (a half-hour ritual of voluntary exasperation of the symptom).

This technique brings to mind Lao Zi's philosophical concept that "a strong action must be given enough space to develop; thus it will eventually undo or exhaust itself." The idea was inspired by the myth about "Yu the Great who governs the waters" (Anonymous 1991, p. 36), who ended the flood in a different way than his father, who had tried in vain—that is, not by building dams to restrain the waters, but by digging canals to make the waters flow where he wanted them to. Decades of clinical experiences by systemic-strategic therapists have shown that prescribing uncontrolled and spontaneous reactions leads these reactions to lose their symptomatic role and disappear (Nardone and Watzlawick 1993, Watzlawick et al. 1967, 1974, Weeks and L'Abate 1982).

After breaking the perceptive-reactive system by applying the three strategic maneuvers just described, we set up a series of concrete experiences to be encountered by the patient under the therapist's guidance. These experiences undisputably prove to the patient that he can now brilliantly overcome any situation previously experienced as terrifying. To make people expose themselves to fear-laden situations after years and years of imprisonment in their own terror, we must again apply the stratagem of "ploughing the sea, unknown to the sky."

But this stratagem is now expressed differently. We make these patients do something they consider frightening while being almost unaware of it. Whether or not these prescriptions are carried out consciously, patients realize after performing them that they have done something they couldn't do before, and without any fear.

A well-planned and correctly conveyed sequence of such prescriptions, which are administered with a decreasing amount of suggestion, will effectively lead patients to overcome all fears of exploration and abandon their solitary isolation. They also receive help to recover their concrete personal resources, which seemed lost forever due to the uncontrollable symptoms.

The therapeutic game ends with an explanation of its rules. We also give detailed explanations of the techniques that have been utilized to win it quickly. This is to make the player (who is both loser and winner) able to play new matches autonomously thanks to his or her new cognitive and behavioral acquisitions.

We now give a detailed, stage by stage exposition of the treatment.

The Treatment Protocol

First Stage

With phobic patients, the first session is an extremely important stage of the treatment. These patients urgently need to find a possibility of resolving their problem and are therefore extremely impressionable, but if they do not immediately have the feeling that they have found the right way, they will go looking for something else. It is very important, therefore, to initiate the essential therapeutic maneuvers as early as possible and quickly get these patients involved in a project for change in order to be able to utilize their receptiveness as a therapeutic element.

On that basis, at the first session, after listening carefully to the patient's description of the problem and using a communication style based on copying the patient's perceptive and expressive modalities, we perform the first therapeutic maneuver: a reframing of the system of interpersonal relationships usually experienced by phobic patients.

The first therapeutic step must be to break the interpersonal system that is maintaining the problem. In the first move, we focus on the individual's perception of this reality, and his usual reactions. We state that his problem, like all his other problems, undoubtedly makes him need the help of other people. But if we want to resolve this dramatic situation, the first step is to realize that the support and help received have no power to change the patient's condition. We tell the patient that he cannot count on the support and protection of others as a solution to his problem; on the contrary, he must begin to consider such help dangerous and damaging, because it can aggravate the problem.

We continue along the same lines, explaining by a kind of suggestive theoretical discussion how the patient's family and friends have become an integral part of the same dysfunctional system and how, being so deeply involved, they can do nothing to change the situation.

By their help and support, friends and family merely confirm the patient's incompetence and dependence. This happens in subtle ways and, if allowed to continue, the situation will only get worse. We stress, however, that the patient cannot, as yet, manage without the help of others.

This initial reframing has the function of channeling the patient's fear and is an incitement to provoke reactions that will break the patient's dysfunctional system of interpersonal relations. By redefining the support and help of other people as something that makes the symptoms increase, we change the patient's perspective on his present relational life, which can no longer be considered an anchor of safety but must be recognized as something damaging and dangerous.

To introduce this new perception in the patient's mind is to initiate a fear of being helped, because being helped means making the symptoms grow more severe. In practice, we redirect the strength of the phobic disorder toward a breakdown of the dysfunctional support network.

It is also very important to stress, in this reframing, that despite everything just said, we do not believe that the patient can initially do without the help of others. This is a paradoxical injunction that usually increases the patient's receptivity; indeed, patients tend to want to prove to the therapist that they can do without the damaging help immediately and collaborate with the therapist to resolve their problems.

After this first therapeutic action, which usually takes up most of the session, we administer the first behavioral prescription to be performed by the patient in the context of everyday life. But we deceitfully state that, for the time being, we are only at an investigative stage, and the assigned homework is only an investigation technique that must be performed to the letter in order to help us acquire a better understanding of the situation. This trick is necessary to keep the patient from trying to measure the effects of the assignment while it is being carried out, because excessive attention toward these effects might inhibit the efficacy of the prescription.

The prescription is worded as follows: "Every time (even if it happens a hundred times a day) you feel a crisis coming, have a moment of panic, feel your anxiety rising, and so on, you will take this log out of your pocket and you will note everything that happens, scrupulously following the enclosed instructions in every detail and filling in each item of this log. At our next session, you will leave me the pages relative to the past week and I will study them."

The logbook is a specially prepared pad that we hand over to the patient together with the prescription; it is made up of boring forms with about ten columns in which to record the date, place, situation, thoughts, symptoms, and the like. At least 5 minutes are required to fill out a form each time a crisis occurs.

These maneuvers had more or less the same effect on the great majority of our cases. The second session would start with the person saying: "Doctor, you must excuse me, I have not done the assignment you gave me. But, oddly, this week I didn't have any crises." Or: "You know, Doctor, it's strange, I have been feeling much better; I had a few critical moments—but, it's incredible, I don't know how to explain it, when I write the log, the anxiety and fear leave me immediately." Moreover, all the patients say that they never asked for help from friends and family that week.

These reports clearly show that the rigid system of perception of reality was broken and the counterproductive social support network was annulled; in other words, the "spell" was broken.

The most probable explanation for this phenomenon seems to be that by shifting the patient's attention from the symptom to the task, the prescribed homework and the reframing performed during the first session constrain the patient against using the usual, unsuccessful, attempted solutions. The obligation to carefully write out thoughts and events induces a completely new reaction to the fear; logging in each episode is such a demanding task that it releases the phobic subject from his original reactions. And inducing the patient to think that seeking and receiving help will aggravate the symptoms puts the patient in the situation of replacing one fear with another, stronger one. But the new fear immobilizes the old one, and thus mobilizes the dysfunctional situation; in other words, we use the strength of fear against fear.

Second Stage

At the second session, after the patient's report on the events of the week, we perform a therapeutic action that reinforces the effect of the previous maneuvers. We redefine the situation: "So the problem is not as great as it seemed, if such a small intervention was enough to change the situation. Your problems, then, are not so impossible nor so inescapable. As you have proven this week, you are truly able to change." And we insist on this redefinition of the problem for the duration of the second session. When the rigid system of dysfunctional reactions is broken, we immediately reinforce the patient's trust in his own abilities. The patient's conscious perception of reality begins to shift from a dysfunctional perspective to a more functional one.

If the patient's responses to the first therapeutic actions have been adequate, we move on to the second stage of the program. Otherwise, we maintain the prescription for another week and repeat the redefinition at the third session, until the desired effect has been reached.

In the last few minutes of the second (or third) session, we assign a new paradoxical behavior prescription: "Since, in the past week(s), you have been so successful at fighting your problem, I am now going to give you an assignment that will seem even stranger and even more absurd than the one you have been performing so far. But, as agreed, you must do it. I believe I have earned a bit of your trust, right? Now, I assume that you have an alarm clock at home, you know the kind that has such an obnoxious ring. Every day, at an agreed hour, you will take this alarm clock and set it to ring half an hour later. During that half hour, you will close yourself in a room of your house, sit in an armchair, force yourself to feel bad, and concentrate on your worst fantasies regarding your problem. You will keep on thinking about your worst fears until you voluntarily produce a crisis of anxiety and panic. You will remain in that state for the rest of the half hour. As soon as the alarm sounds, you will turn it off and discontinue the exercise, stop the thoughts and sensations you have provoked, go and wash your face, and resume your usual daily activities."

This prescription has two kinds of possible effects. The first is, "Doctor, I really wasn't able to become fully absorbed in the situation; I tried, but it all seemed so ridiculous that I wound up laughing. Oddly, instead of making me feel bad, it was relaxing." The second is, "Doctor, I succeeded so well in doing the assignment that I felt the same sensations as before coming to you. It was very painful; I cried sometimes; then, luckily, the alarm sounded and it was all over."

Most patients in both response groups had experienced no moments of crisis outside the half-hour assignment, and some patients had only had infrequent episodes of anxiety that were easily brought under control.

At the next session, after the patient's report on the effects of the prescription, we again take steps to redefine the situation in terms of positive change. In the case of the first type of response, our redefinition will be as follows: "As you have had a chance to see, your problem can be alleviated by provoking it voluntarily; it's a paradox, but you know, sometimes our mind works in paradoxical ways rather than according to common sense. You are starting to learn not to fall into the trap of your disorder and your attempted solutions that complicate problems instead of resolving them." The entire session proceeds on the same tone.

With the second type of response, the redefinition is worded as follows: "Very good. You are learning to modulate and manage your disorder. Just as you can voluntarily provoke the symptoms, you can also limit them and make them disappear. The more you are able to provoke them during the half hour, the better will you succeed in controlling them during the rest of the day." And so on, for the duration of the session.

Thus, in both cases, our redefinition of the effect of the prescription focuses on reinforcing the patient's awareness and trust in the ongoing change, and on the fact that he or she is learning new and efficacious strategies for dealing with possible future fears.

The patient has received incontrovertible, practical proof that the work undertaken together with the specialist is efficacious. This creates an exceptional collaboration and leads to further progressive changes in the patient's perception of reality. We also take care to ascribe the merit for the change to the patient's personal capacities, while presenting the therapist as a strategist who uses particular techniques to bring out something that the patient already has but does not know how to use. We always focus on increasing the patient's personal competence and self-esteem. This consideration is greatly motivating for patients who have always considered themselves incompetent (and whose family and friends have confirmed this opinion); it also frees the intervention from the possibility of being considered a sort of magic.

After a few weeks, the situation has radically changed; in almost all the cases considered in this book, the gripping and immobilizing symptoms disappeared at this point. However, the patients cannot be considered completely recovered. In this phase, it becomes extremely important to reduce any euphoria and warn the patient against the dangers of too swift a recovery. The watchword now is "go slow" (Fisch et al. 1982b). It is essential for the patients to slow down and realize that if they step too much on the accelerator they may go off the road and fall back into their old problems. The important thing now is to consolidate what we have obtained.

Third Stage

The next step, having reached this stage of the therapy, is to plan indirect behavioral prescriptions involving the patient's gradual exposure to a progressive sequence of anxiety-producing situations. This is somewhat analogous to systematic desensitization, with the difference that, for each indirect prescription, we add some suggestion that helps the patient carry out the anxiety-laden task.

The following, for example, is a typical prescription: "Very well. Since you have been very good at carrying out everything I have asked you to do so far, you will now be able to do even more. As Robert Frost said once, the best way to come out of it is to walk through it; therefore, we are now going to walk right through your fears. Between now and our next session, you will do exactly what I am about to ask you. On Saturday at 10 A.M. you will dress to go out, walk to your door, and, before opening it, make a pirouette. Then you will open the door, go out, close the door, make another pirouette, walk downstairs to the front door of your building, make another pirouette, open the door, and go out; then you will do another pirouette and start walking to the center of town. Go to the fruit and vegetable market and look for the biggest, reddest, and ripest apple you can find. Buy only that apple and bring it to me here at the office. Keep in mind that I will be busy, so knock on my door, and I will open it. You will leave me the apple; I will have it for lunch. We will meet again at the next session."

The result of this prescription is that people smilingly knock on the office door holding out a paper bag with a beautiful apple inside. Not only that; after performing this strange task, they usually start going out alone without fear, venturing gradually farther and farther. As soon as these subjects, who had grown accustomed to the idea of feeling uneasy every time they ventured to leave their safe places on their own, experience this peaceful, almost funny, astonishingly simple kind of exploration, they are released from their fear.

The prescription enables patients to perform a frightening task because their minds have been distracted from the more anxiety-laden task that must be performed in order to carry out the whole assignment. Once it is done, however, patients realize that they have truly overcome their fear. They understand the trick, of course, but they have also proved to themselves by this undeniable practical action that they really can overcome their own difficulties.

Classical behavioral desensitizations often fail because patients refuse to carry out direct behavioral prescriptions; by means of a kind trick, we have, in contrast, obtained the performance of prescriptions that would have failed if they had been presented on their own. In this kind of maneuver, like jugglers and magicians who shift the observer's attention while they perform their tricks, we find ways to get around immobilizing fears. In our work with the large group of phobic patients considered here, we have devised many prescriptions of this kind. Readers will find several concrete instances described in the two case examples presented in the Appendix.

In the third stage, the treatment evolves through the performance of direct behavioral prescriptions, each according to an agreed list of anxiety-laden situations. Just like in the initial stage of therapy, after each prescription we take care to redefine the patients' real abilities as proved by their overcoming situations that would have thrown them into a crisis before. Moreover, as the treatment evolves, the suggestions that accompany prescriptions are gradually diminished, to a point in time after which we only give direct behavioral prescriptions using dialogic (instead of injunctive) language as in the previous parts of therapy.

Through this procedure, we usually reach a moment when the patients themselves state that they now feel capable of dealing, without problems, with all situations previously experienced as frightening.

Fourth Stage: The Last Session

The last session is the final brushstroke and the appropriate picture frame for the accomplished work. Its objective is a permanent consolidation of the patient's self-esteem and personal autonomy. Toward this end, we proceed with a detailed recapitulation and explanation of the therapeutic process and the techniques utilized, showing how these function, and emphasizing the fact that the change has occurred thanks to the patient's personal gifts. The therapist has only activated these already-present personal characteristics, and has added nothing, because that would be impossible.

In conclusion, we state that the patient has now learned to make good use of his personal gifts and therefore no longer needs the therapist. We agree on the follow-up procedure, and therapy ends.

STRATEGY AND STRATAGEMS FOR RESOLVING
THE PANIC ATTACK SYNDROME

As we observed in the previous chapter, the severe forms of phobic disorder described here are similar or identical in some aspects and substantially different in others. Within the logic of a strategic intervention designed to break such rigid and recursive cybernetic systems, it is very
important to consider the differences between various forms of disorder;
the treatment protocol must be flexibly adapted to these differences through
specific maneuvers, while for pathology with the same structure of attempted solutions it remains unvaried.

Our therapeutic strategy for treating the panic attack syndrome includes some of the techniques utilized in our treatment of agoraphobia,
but with the difference that we initially focus on the specific attempted
solutions of this particular perceptive-reactive system.

The two attempted solutions that maintain this problem instead of
resolving it are help seeking and, more particularly, the patient's obsessive
attempt to control the psychophysiological expressions of the phobic symptom, with the obvious result of increasing the symptom.

Our first technique consists of changing the direction of this obsessive effort. Toward this end, we utilize a reframing based on techniques of
confusion, paradox, and symptom shifting (reframing and prescription of
the usefulness of the symptom).

Here again we find analogies with the oriental art of stratagems. Our
maneuver employs one known as "making the water muddy in order
to catch the fish" or "making noise to the West in order to attack from
the East." In other words, against the obsession of control, we utilize
a technique that encourages the obsession, while redirecting it against
a new objective prescribed by the therapist; the situation, as a result,
becomes even more confused. We create mental confusion by using
arguments that seem even more complicated and elaborate than the
patient's own, and instruct the patient to ponder something that, to him,
seems absurd—the positive value of his symptoms. To this tactic we
add the injunction of reframing messages in metaphorical form (first
prescription in metaphorical form). As an effect of the confusion we
have produced, the patient will try to hang on to the metaphor, which,
however, will subvert the hyperrational logic of attempting to control
reactions.

After these first two maneuvers, we prescribe the paradoxical ritual (a half-hour of the symptom) already described in our treatment of agoraphobia. Then, utilizing the control fantasies that are typical of these disorders, we train patients to use paradox as a technique for controlling any future appearances of the symptom. This stratagem, which puts a definite stop to the attempted solution of listening to oneself and checking one's own reactions, is analogous to the ancient stratagem of "removing the firewood from under the cauldron," that is, getting rid of what kept the fire going and the water boiling.

Having reached this stage, we proceed with a paradoxical injunction of relapses. As an effect of paradoxical logic, the prescribed relapses punctually fail to occur. In the ancient art of strategy, this technique was defined as the stratagem of "throwing the brick in order to get the jade back"; this definition clearly conveys the idea that encouraging an obsessive reaction can lead to its disappearance.

Here too, the game ends with a disclosure of the tactical secrets and techniques utilized in its course.

Treatment Protocol

First Stage

As usual, our first meeting with the patient is focused on acquiring power of intervention by creating an attractive atmosphere of personal contact and acceptance. This is achieved through the usual techniques of strategic communication.

With patients who suffer from panic attacks, it is particularly important to express support and acceptance of their often objectively unmotivated fears and fixations. Otherwise, we would immediately create a counterproductive relationship. The therapist who tries to make patients realize that their phobic convictions are absurd in order to make them change their minds is attempting the same unsuccessful tactic as people inspired by common sense. On the contrary, the attitude that has proved most productive in our experience is based on the paradoxical logic that is expressed by showing active acceptance of the patient's fears, seriously considering the idea that the patient's persuasions of being ill might be accurate, and even finding some justification for the patient's convictions on the basis that they might fulfill some positive function.

Toward the end of the session we offer an elaborate, tortuous, pedantic, and unclear reframing of the presenting problem, quoting facts and reflections leading to the demonstration that such disorders might either fulfill an important role or represent a crucial function in the patient's personality. Indeed, they may be signs of a special quality, a gift reserved only for those rare beings who are more aware, more sensitive than other people. "In nature, as you know, if something exists or persists over time within a complex system, this means that that something necessarily fulfills an important role within that system. If it were not so, that something would tend to disappear. Now, I wonder, what could be the positive role or function of your disorder in the natural, complex system that is your organism?" We conclude with the suggestion that the patient think about this matter in the course of the week.

At the end of the session, while walking the patient to the door, we tell the following little story: "An ancient tale recounts how, once upon a time, an ant asked a centipede, 'Can you tell me how you can walk so well with a hundred feet? Can you explain how you are able to control them all at the same time?' The centipede started to think about that and could no longer walk."

After this brief narrative, we say good-bye and invite the patient to think about the meaning of the story.

In practical terms, we redefine the presenting symptom by sowing the doubt that it may have a positive role or important function that needs to be investigated. This further complicates the patient's already intricate network of thoughts, leading it to a paradoxical aggravation, and simultaneously turns the patient's thoughts toward a new, surprising perspective of analysis of this reality. And finally, we reframe the attempted obsessive solution of listening to and trying to control oneself by employing the suggestion of a metaphor.

These initial maneuvers usually produce the effects seen in the subsequent stages.

Second Stage

At the second session, the patients usually report two kinds of reactions: "You know, doctor, I spent the whole week thinking about what purpose my strange ideas and actions might have, but I still don't have a clue. However, my mind has felt less cluttered in the past few days." Or:

"Doctor, I think I have understood that my actions really serve some purpose, though I can't say what; however, I have felt a little better, with fewer fixations. And, you know, I thought a lot about that centipede and could really recognize myself in it. Yes, I really am acting like that centipede who could no longer walk."

Thus, the paradoxical reframing had the effect of mitigating the obsessive tension—even if only slightly—by complicating it even further, but also by implying that the disorder might have some possible, obscure, mysterious, and positive meaning. As a result, the patient's attention was shifted onto something different from the usual chain of thoughts based on fears. The lack of usefulness was not identified by the patients, but their impossible quest mitigated the obsessive mechanism of attempted solutions such as, for example, "trying not to think" and thereby thinking even more, or "always trying to control the body" and thereby increasing the panic symptoms. As mentioned earlier, a voluntary effort to do something spontaneous will inhibit the spontaneity and make it impossible to reach what one is making every effort to reach. Reducing even a small part of that mechanism quickly relieves some of the tension involved.

After listening to the patient's report, we reinforce the hypothesis that the symptoms may have a positive functional role for the personality of the patient by means of a further complicated and contorted series of ideas and suppositions. In the last few minutes of the session, we assign a paradoxical behavior prescription directed toward the patient's dysfunctional attempted solution of control. This is the half-hour ritual with the alarm clock that has been described in the previous section.

At the third session, the patients' reports are usually the same as for agoraphobic patients. The patients were either able to feel bad during the half hour, or they relaxed and even had positive thoughts. In both cases the patients usually report a decrease in the panic symptoms.

Without giving any explicit explanations, we narrate the metaphor of Yu the Great (p. 45) and prescribe that the half-hour ritual be increased to 45 minutes a day.

At the following session, most patients report that their symptoms have diminished again. Almost all patients, moreover, say that they have not succeeded in their attempts to feel bad during the prescribed 45 minutes; on the contrary, they started to feel relaxed.

We increase the prescribed time to one hour a day and again invite the subjects to think about the centipede. While saying goodbye, we reinforce our message with another metaphor or anecdote, for example: "Once upon a time, a prince was fascinated by the flight of birds. He tied two birds together so that they could fly better. The birds, then, had four wings, but they could no longer fly."

Third Stage

By the fourth session, most patients report that they have felt considerably better and have experienced fewer episodes of panic. Many patients also declare that they spent a lot of time thinking about the centipede and the prince of the second story, and understood that they had also fallen into a similar trap. They cannot explain their improvement. How can the panic attacks possibly have decreased or, in some cases, disappeared completely?

At this point we redefine the situation with a general explanation of the trick we have used; in other words, we explain how paradoxes, in addition to producing problems, can also be utilized to unseat problems. We emphasize that there is a clear possibility of resolving the patient's problem by using this alternative kind of logic. Utilizing injunctive language, we prescribe the exasperation of what we want to repress, so as to make it disappear by a paradoxical effect. We emphasize the fact that the patient has now acquired a new and efficient instrument for fighting the fear.

However, we also declare that it is now essential to slow down the process of change. "If you step too hard on the accelerator, you might go off the road." We also tell the patient: "I think we can anticipate some relapses during the coming weeks, because some disorders can overbearingly return after having disappeared. Indeed, I believe that you will almost certainly have a proper relapse. Whatever happens, keep on doing what you have learned to do." Predictably, the following week only very few patients report having had an immediate relapse; the majority come back and say that they have felt yet a little better, with fewer fixed thoughts about feeling sick, and almost completely free of fear.

In both cases, we give the patients the following prescription: "Good. Now that we have switched off those mechanisms, we can start using your sensitivity and your great awareness in positive ways. During the next few days, when you go out, I want you to do what anthropologists usually do when they go out to study a certain culture. They carefully observe people's behavior: the way they move, the way they speak, the way they act, and so on. On the basis of such observations, anthropologists try to understand people and the rules that govern their behavior, their society, and their culture. I want you to do just that: observe and study the people you see outside, the people you meet. I want you to strive to understand what kind of people they are by the way they act. I am sure that, with your sensitivity and awareness, you will discover interesting things. At our next session, you will tell me about your discoveries."

This prescription, which is called "the prescription of the anthropologist," has the aim of shifting the patients' attention from listening to themselves to listening to others. It helps them to stop paying too much attention to their own actions and to what happens inside them (the latter mechanism often works as a self-fulfilling prophecy), by shifting their attention toward the observation and anthropological study of other people.

At the following session, most patients report that they have suffered no relapse, and give the therapist a lively description of many kinds of human behavior. It is sometimes surprising to hear what a mass of information and reflections the patients report. Some have even observed symptomatic behavior in others, or have discovered something they would never have imagined—that many people have problems.

The whole session is spent on reflections stimulated by the patient's report and on incentives to continue doing research on other people. By expressing favorable judgments, we reinforce the abilities shown by the patient in performing this not very easy task and point out that these abilities can be very useful in one's interactions with other people.

In some patients, the obsessive situation has been reduced to a minimum by the sixth or the seventh session; we therefore proceed to redefine the situation, emphasizing the abilities shown by the patient in fighting the problem, which has been overcome owing to the patient's exceptional collaboration with us. In these cases, the therapist starts to lengthen the intervals between sessions, with the clear intention of strengthening the patient's personal autonomy by showing a greater trust in the patient's new abilities. At the following sessions, we proceed with further positive redefinitions of the situations and the changes obtained until the end of therapy is reached.

In most cases, however, at the session after the second week of the "prescription of the anthropologist," the situation will look different. The patients have reduced their moments of panic to a minimum and are no longer the slaves of their fixations about the possibility of feeling sick, but they frequently still have a tendency to think too much, complicating things, making them difficult and transforming them into sources of worry. Thus, even though the patients no longer present phobic behavior, they still have obsessive inclinations in their analyses of reality, with a propensity to think too much and act too little.

We have devised a particular form of treatment for such cases: the prescription of the "magic formula." This is the assignment: for every complicated rumination, the patient must write the following sentence five times: "Think little and learn by doing!" The task is assigned without explaining the meaning of this phrase.

Very few patients carry out this prescription. This is why we have ironically dubbed it the "magic formula." Almost all patients report that, at the thought of having to write this sentence, they felt liberated from having to think and rethink about things, and began to act with more ease and less prior ruminations.

It seems to us that this intervention is effective in giving the final thrust against obsessive systems of perception and reaction toward reality, because of the irony it implies. The person who tries to perform this task, after having made significant advances in fighting problems during the past weeks, will recognize it as a form of self-mockery. The person will avoid this potential self-humiliation, and in avoiding it will also avoid the residual obsessiveness. At this point we move on to progressive positive redefinitions of the change achieved and of the capability the patient has demonstrated in confronting the problem, lengthening the interval between sessions until we reach the end of the treatment.

Fourth Stage

In the final session for patients with panic attacks, we follow exactly the same procedure as for agoraphobic patients.

STRATEGY AND STRATAGEMS FOR RESOLVING COMPOSITE AGORAPHOBIA AND PANIC ATTACK SYNDROMES

As we have described in Chapter 2, when a symptomatology persists over a long time, it is often joined by other complementary symptomatologies. That is the case with patients who develop a panic attack syndrome on the basis of an agoraphobic syndrome or vice versa.

Such composite disorders are the sum of two specific phobic disorders, but the sum of the parts is not equal to the whole. The whole is what biologists define as an "emerging quality."

Here we confront perceptive-reactive systems that have their own particular ways of functioning. If we apply a treatment protocol that does not take this into account, we will obtain nothing but minimal results or total failures.

Our experience has shown that to resolve such composite problems effectively, we must understand which of the two syndromes is the fundamental one. If we find that the dominant perceptive-reactive system is agoraphobic, then our intervention must focus on breaking and changing the vicious circle between the attempted solutions of avoidance and help seeking and the persistence of the problem that is sustained by those attempted solutions. If, on the other hand, we find that the panic attack syndrome is the dominant one, then we must focus on changing the attempted solutions that typically maintain the problem in this kind of disorder—in other words, help seeking and the obsessive control of reactions.

In treating these problem typologies, we follow a treatment protocol that is itself a sort of "emerging quality" obtained by joining the two protocols presented above. During the first stages of the treatment, we give priority to discovering which perceptive-reactive system is the dominant one. This diagnosis can be made on the basis of the patient's responses to our initial therapeutic maneuvers. For example, if the patient responds to the log prescription by bringing back a notebook full of detailed, meticulous notes, we will know that the perceptive-reactive system we are dealing with is based on control; therefore, we will act on the hypothesis that the panic attack system is the prevailing one.

If, on the contrary, the patient reacts to the log prescription by bringing back very few notes or none and reporting that he has experienced fewer symptoms over the past few days, then we will know that we are dealing with an agoraphobic dominance.

In conclusion, once we have discovered the prevalent pathology we follow the specific protocol for that problem, also introducing a few maneuvers suitable for breaking the added symptomatology. It is important to keep in mind, however, that we only reach a radical solution to the problem when a real change in the dominant perceptive-reactive system has been obtained.

STRATEGY AND STRATAGEMS FOR RESOLVING OBSESSIVE-COMPULSIVE SYNDROMES

As we described in the previous chapter, the typical perceptive-reactive system of compulsive-obsessive syndromes is maintained by the attempted solutions of avoidance and control of anxiety-laden situations through obsessive propitiatory or protective rituals.

The first stratagem for rupturing this dysfunctional cybernetic system is to "catch the fish by making the water muddy," in other words, a therapeutic reframing maneuver based on confusion, paradox, and symptom-shifting techniques. The second stratagem is to prescribe the half-hour-long paradoxical ritual.

The third stratagem (a variant of the second) is to prescribe that the patient repeat the obsessive rituals for a specific high number of times each time the original ritual appears. This technique is useful for gaining control of the symptom and steering the force of the symptom toward self-annulment. The maneuvers that come after are a series of counter-rituals devised specifically for each patient and prescribed to make the patient deal with all the fear-laden situations in a progressive sequence that leads up to the concluding ritual that represents the final victory over the symptoms and the complete resolution of the problem. This final ritual must function as a true initiation or rite of passage from one state to another in the patient's life. It must, therefore, be a ritual sequence that analogously symbolizes the defeat of the obscure illness and the patient's victory over fear.

Here again, we conclude the therapeutic game by revealing all its tactical secrets and the apparently "magical" tricks that have been performed. This is to give the patient awareness of and complete credit for having effected the changes and recovered personal resources.

The Treatment Protocol

First Stage

As usual, the focus of our first meeting with the patient is on creating an atmosphere of acceptance and interpersonal contact in order to acquire powers of intervention.

With obsessive-compulsive patients, it is extremely important to support and accept their fixations and their contorted and sometimes disagreeable rituals. Otherwise, the therapist would immediately establish a counterproductive relationship. The therapist who tries to persuade patients that their compulsions are absurd, as an attempt to make them control their compulsion to perform rituals and change their manner of action, behaves just like people motivated by "plain common sense" unsuccessfully do with phobic patients. The logic of common sense, when applied to things that do not function according to that logic, has the effect of producing no change at all in obsessive-compulsive patients; it only gives them the impression of not having been understood, and makes them think that they really must be sick since they are unable to act like "normal" people.

The attitude that has proved most productive with this type of patient, as with patients who suffer from panic attacks, is based on paradoxical logic. This is expressed during the first session by actively showing acceptance of the patients' odd fixations, seriously considering the possibility that their absurd convictions might make sense, and even looking for some justification for these convictions on the basis that they might serve some useful purpose.

When defining the problem and agreeing on the objectives of the treatment, we apply the usual communication strategy of learning and utilizing the logic and the language of the patient and avoiding any expression of opinions that might be opposed to the patient's point of view. On the contrary, the patient's point of view is endorsed and reinforced during the rest of the session.

The next step is the "utility reframing" described above. Moreover, we redefine the compulsive rituals as too important for the patient, at least for the time being, to be taken away; the rituals must instead be performed without any control at all.

A few examples can help to clarify what we mean by compulsive rituals:

A young accountant, whose obsessive fear of making mistakes unendingly forced him to keep checking and rechecking the progressive numbering of invoices and other material, finally collapsed one day and had to take temporary leave from work.

A young man, obsessed by a fear that he might be homosexual, daily subjected himself to marathon-like sessions of watching pornographic movies and reading pornographic magazines with the intention of measuring the comparative excitement he felt toward the feminine or the masculine sex.

Obsessed by the conviction that she had run over a pedestrian, a woman repeatedly had to return to the place of the presumed "crime" escorted by another person who had to reassure her that her belief was unfounded.

Obsessively convinced that his wife was being unfaithful to him, a husband found contorted support for this belief in any not even remotely connected event. Thus, he had to follow his wife everywhere, checking all her movements.

A young girl ritually had to check several times that all faucets, doors, and windows were closed before being able to go to bed. Later in the night, she would wake up and have to perform the whole ritual again.

Confirming the importance of the rituals is clearly both a realistic and a paradoxical strategic maneuver that makes it possible for us to gain control over these rituals.

These first two therapeutic moves are usually reported to produce the following effects: Reframing the problem as being useful usually produces the same responses as with patients who suffer from panic attacks; thinking about the symptom's positive role produces a slight decrease in the obsessions, whether or not the patient has been able to guess what that positive role might be. Redefining the compulsive rituals as something important that must not be restrained usually produces a significant reduction of tension and sometimes a slight decrease in the frequency of the rituals.

A spontaneous, uncontrollable symptomatology is transformed into something useful and important, which must not be repressed, at least for the time being. This perspective is a first element of discomposure in the dysfunctional equilibrium of the patient's perceptive-reactive system.

This change of perspective concentrates the patient's attention upon something other than the usual; instead of striving to check the compulsive forces and trying not to think or act in compulsive ways, the patient is made to concentrate upon the possible usefulness and present importance of the symptoms. Thus the obsessive mechanism of "attempted solutions" is mitigated as an effect of the paradox.

As we have said before, an active effort to do something spontaneous will inhibit the spontaneity. In obsessive persons, attempts to control rituals and fears produce the opposite effect of maintaining and incrementing them. Even a slight disconnection in this mechanism is enough to relieve the tension.

Second Stage

At the second session, after the patient's report, we reinforce the hypothesis that the symptoms may have a positive functional role for the patient's personality. This result is obtained by presenting a further series of complicated and contorted ideas and suppositions until it becomes time, in the last few minutes of the session, to prescribe two tasks: the half-hour with the alarm clock, and a second one that we shall now describe. It is another paradoxical behavior prescription, but this one has the objective of directly influencing compulsive behavior. It is a prescription of the symptom, worded as follows: "On the basis of what we have done so far, I am now going to give you a specific assignment that you must perform without any questions or explanations, because it will help to dispel your doubts regarding the positive function of your disorder; therefore, you must accomplish it on your own. I will provide explanations only later. Whenever you find that you must do those things that you feel that you must do, I don't want you to resist and not do them. Instead, I want you to repeat them voluntarily ten times—exactly ten times! You can avoid it. But if you do them one time, do them ten times. No more, no less."

This prescription must be given in the form of a hypnotic suggestion, describing exactly the behavior to be carried out in slow, rhythmical, repetitive, redundant language.

To give a few examples of the contents of the prescriptions, the accountant who kept checking that the invoices were numbered correctly was asked to go over them ten times each time he felt the need to check; the young woman of the nocturnal rituals had to repeat every ritual ten times; people who wash themselves continually for fear of dirt have to wash ten times; the young man obsessed by fear of being homosexual had to look ten times at all his magazines and the most disturbing parts of the films. And the woman who was terrorized by the thought of having run over a pedestrian had to return ten times to the hypothetical scene of the crime every time she felt the doubt.

To prescribe something that one usually tries to repress will deprive the symptom of its symptomatic quality.

In fact, the most frequent report at the third session was: "Doctor, I carried out the assignment you gave me, but I wasn't able to do it ten times. Sometimes I couldn't do it at all. You told me that I would understand the function of my problems, but I still don't understand anything!" Some clients reported that they had been unable to repeat the actions and rituals because they never had felt the need to do them and could not force themselves to do something they didn't want to do; those patients also stated that they still had not understood the positive role of their problems.

As for the half-hour prescription, the most frequent report was that while obstinately trying to feel miserable, the patients inexplicably began to have many positive thoughts and ideas.

After these reports, we again stress the importance of performing that specific act exactly ten times during the following week, and emphasize the fact that the patient is beginning to gain control over the situation. Still without offering any explanations, we also prescribe the daily half hour of deliberate provocation of symptoms, subdividing it into 5 minutes, six times a day, at set times.

Third Stage

At the fourth session, most patients report that they had felt decidedly better and had only experienced a few episodes of obsessiveness and repetitions of actions, and that every time they had felt the impulse to engage in their symptomatic behavior, the need to carry it through had disappeared as soon as they started performing it deliberately. Many of these patients said, moreover, that during the 5 minutes six times a day when they made efforts to think about all their fears and fixations the fears and fixations did not appear, and many positive things to do came to mind instead.

At that point we redefined the situation, explaining the main aspects of the trick we had utilized and how just as the "be spontaneous" paradox can cause problems, it can also be used to unsettle certain other problems, in this case their own. We particularly insisted on the idea that there is a clear possibility of resolving these problems as soon as the logic of our reactions to them has changed.

But after that, we also declared, as usual, that it was now necessary to slow down the process of change: "If we step too heavily on the accelerator, we will go off the road." We also predicted that there would be a re-lapse in the following week.

We direct the patients to perform the paradoxical ritual of thinking voluntarily about all their worst fears for 3 minutes, three times a day. Finally, we prescribe the following: "If you repeat an action, you will have to repeat it fifteen times, not even once more nor once less. Of course, maybe you won't have to do any repetitions, but if you do it once, you will have to repeat it fifteen times, not even once less nor once more."

Here, too, in the following week, very few patients report that the anticipated relapse had occurred; the majority come back and report that there had been no relapse; instead, they had felt yet a little better, with fewer fixed thoughts and almost no repeated action repertoires.

For both kinds of reports, the next move, after redefining the situation still further and again stressing the clear possibility of changing and resolving the problem, is to predict another relapse—a somewhat lighter one for the patients who had suffered a relapse; as for the others, we predict the relapse that had not occurred the week before.

Having reached this stage of the therapy, in most cases we proceed to prescribe the anthropologist (described above), in order to shift the patient's attention toward the study of other people.

This shift of attention helps patients to avoid paying too much attention to themselves and their own actions, a mechanism that usually functions as a self-fulfilling prophecy and leads to compulsive reactions to realities that are experienced as menacing.

Fourth Stage

In our less complicated cases, the obsessive situations are reduced to a minimum by the sixth or seventh session; therefore, we proceed to rede-fine the situation, emphasizing the capability shown by the patients in fighting their problems through their exceptional collaboration with the therapist. In those cases, we start to lengthen the intervals between sessions with the obvious intention of reinforcing personal autonomy and showing greater trust in the patient's newly acquired abilities.

At the following sessions, we proceed with further positive redefinitions of the situation and the change that had been obtained, until we reach the end of the therapy.

With more complicated cases, on the other hand, this is the time for counter-rituals. The patients have reduced their repertoires of obsessive actions to a minimum and are no longer enslaved by their fixations, but they still have a frequent tendency to think too much, complicating issues, and to be very insecure. Therefore, even when these ideas are no longer forcing desolating ritual compulsions upon the patients, it seems necessary to do something that will put them in the position of completely abandoning their frightening and obsessive ideas. Otherwise, these patients may suffer a relapse after some time because their perception of menacing realities has not switched to alternative perceptions.

For such situations, we need to devise a "rite of passage" from the state of a person who is afraid to the state of a person who has overcome fear. The structure of such complex prescriptions is devised by planning the performance of a series of actions that signify a final symbolic victory over fear. Such a sequence of actions, with its conclusive result, functions like well-known tribal rituals of initiation and passage from one social position to a higher one.

For example, a patient who had presented a phobic obsession about dirt, especially excrement, was assigned the following conclusive ritual. We asked her to study all the different typologies of animal excrement that she could find in the vicinity of her country house. Later, she was told to arm herself with a shovel and scoop up the most significant of the excrements, take it home, and flush it down the toilet. That way she could definitively free herself of the symbolic object and of the remaining fears and fixations. (Other examples of creative counter-rituals will be described in the Appendix.)

This kind of prescription as the conclusion of a therapeutic battling process against phobic obsessions and consequent compulsive rituals has, in most cases, the effect of a true liberation and passage from one life situation to another. To reach the conclusive counter-ritual, we sometimes have to proceed gradually with a progressive series of counter-rituals, but very often one well-designed counter-ritual is sufficient.

The liberating "magic" of this maneuver is that it utilizes the same ritual structure as the symptom, in the opposite direction. It is carried out in the engaging form of a sort of initiatory test of courage. This ritual, even more than others, must be prescribed through injunctive-suggestive communication; otherwise, only the rare patient will carry out such apparently absurd sequences of actions.

At that point, as in the cases previously described, we proceed with progressive, positive redefinitions of the now-tangible change and the patient's proven capability of dealing with the problem, giving all the credit for the change that has occurred to the patient. Then we lengthen the intervals between sessions, until we reach the conclusion of the therapy.

The Last Session

In our last session, we do exactly as described in the previous sections: put the final picture frame around the accomplished work of art.

STRATEGY AND STRATAGEMS FOR RESOLVING PHOBIC-HYPOCHONDRIAC SYNDROMES

As described in Chapter 2, the attempted solutions that maintain the dysfunctional perceptive-reactive system typical of hypochondriac fixation syndromes are (1) help seeking and (2) attempting to control the presumed illness by obsessively searching for a definite diagnosis. Therefore, the stratagems for breaking and changing this type of cybernetic system that we developed in the course of our research intervention are, apart from a few variations, the same as for intervention on the composite panic attack and agoraphobia syndrome.

REFLECTIONS AT THE MARGINS OF TECHNIQUES

> *No night is so long that it does not see the day.*
>
> Shakespeare, *Hamlet*

From what has been said so far, it should be clear that the quick, effective solution of severe phobic disorders can be achieved by a specific, rigorous therapeutic intervention that is expressed in a preestablished sequence of maneuvers studied for each case and according to the type of disorder. These maneuvers and sequences have resulted from our research-intervention and from our formulation of the constructs *perceptive-reactive system* and *interaction between persistence and attempted solution of the problem*. These treatment protocols form not a rigid and immutable methodology but rather a flexible instrument that systematically guides the therapist toward the resolution of problems. To be effective, this instrument must be adapted to the patients' different personalities, contexts, and language typologies. Studying, acquiring, and using the patient's language is one of the essential premises of the strategic approach of adapting the therapist and the treatment to the patient and not the patient to the treatment and the therapist.

These protocols should therefore be considered something like the strategies of moves for winning a chess game quickly. Both in chess and in therapy, we proceed by successive moves, trying to anticipate the other player's intentions, reacting to his countermoves by further countermoves, until we reach checkmate. But obviously, however isomorphic the sequences of moves may be, each game is always new with respect to other games.

Moreover, even if the sequence of therapeutic maneuvers may seem to be the same, every therapy is a new therapy because we find within it original interactive situations produced by the interaction between the therapist and the particular features of each patient.

The protocols must, therefore, be used flexibly and at times creatively and be adapted to the specific characteristics of the person who comes asking for help. The same maneuver can be expressed in very different communicative formulations according to whether the patient, for example, is a hyperrational or an imaginative and poetic kind of person. To be effective, all injunctions in brief strategic therapy must be expressed in the patient's language. The same sequence of specific maneuvers can therefore take on a very different coloration each time it is applied. What remains unvaried is the structure of the intervention, while what is always changing is the interaction between therapist and patient.

We proceed as we have described, studying the persisting character of the presented problem (the functioning of its perceptive-reactive system); we decide on objectives, study strategies, and adapt our typology of communication and therapeutic interaction to the patients' characteristics. The objectives and general strategy usually remain unvaried in interventions on disorders based on isomorphic typologies of problem persistence, but the therapeutic communication and interaction change each time, as they adapt to the patients' particular perceptive, cognitive, and relational features.

The personality of the therapist is a crucial factor in this kind of therapy. The therapist is both the director and the principal actor of the movie. He or she must possess refined technical preparation, great methodological rigorousness, a lively creativity, and great mental flexibility. In other words, the therapist must simultaneously be a scientist and an artist

(Keeney 1991), like those great musicians who are able to compose and also give the best performance of their own compositions. Like a masterfully performed piece of music, brief strategic therapy seems amazingly simple. But in therapy, as in music, behind the apparent simplicity of a performance there lies a complex thread of subtle and refined maneuvers that are the fruit of long study and laborious experimentation.

4

Efficacy of the Treatment

It is a cause of great unhappiness to be of no use at all, but to be useful in everything is no smaller cause of unhappiness.

Baldasar Gracian

THE EPISTEMOLOGICAL VALIDITY OF A MODEL OF THERAPY

It is important to show how our treatment protocol has enabled us to achieve remarkably and in some aspects even surprisingly effective results.

Toward this end, we have researched the outcome of our interventions in order to prove that the results we obtained in the above-described cases are neither accidental nor limited to those cases only. We consider it necessary to present an empirical account of our therapeutic outcomes and a statistical elaboration of our data in accordance with the methods prescribed in the literature of psychological research.

As explained (but it may be useful to emphasize this concept again), when a type of intervention produces speedy, effective, and concrete changes in a certain problem, the strategy and tactics of the intervention will be appreciated for their technical efficacy. At the same time, experiences of resolutive interventions on problems of the same kind lead to advancements in our knowledge about that type of problem.

And when, as in our case, the replication of results has endured repeated applications of the model to a statistically significant sample of subjects, we may infer that this formalized typology of intervention is not only an efficient technical instrument but also a methical and scientific procedure for intervention in specific problems.

According to the epistemological criteria of contemporary science, we consider a model "scientific" if it has the characteristics of efficacy, repeatability, and predictability (Giannattasio and Nencini 1983). Besides having proved to be efficacious and replicable, this model, based on the preparation of specific tactics and techniques for the specific, stage-by-stage objectives of the treatment, has also proved to be predictive. The procedure and the order of development of the treatment are based on the prediction of a limited number of responses to each unit of intervention. On the basis of the patient's response to each intervention, we proceed with the next specific maneuver. The process of therapy is like an interactive dance between the therapist and the patient, within a preestablished script of possible movements and countermovements.

As its name implies, a "strategic" approach is based on the preparation of strategies that, like those of a chess game, provide for the predictive planning of moves. However, such strategic plans can be changed during the game, so that one can adapt, with specific variants, to possible variations within the game.

In Bateson's language, the regulation and planning of this model also provide for the self-correction of its rules.

EFFICACY OF THE THERAPY

The evaluation of the effects or results obtained in therapy is one of the thorniest issues in psychotherapy. Much of the difficulty arises from the different schools of psychotherapy having different criteria for establishing the efficacy of therapies; this is an unavoidable consequence of diverse theoretical perspectives, which at times assume opposing positions.

For example, for a Freudian psychoanalyst, the treatment is efficacious when it leads the patient to overcome the Oedipus complex; a Jungian analyst will see the efficacy of therapy in the achievement of personal individuation; for a behaviorist, therapeutic success is represented by the extinction of the behavioral symptoms; for a family therapist, success lies in the reorganization of the family system; for a brief-strategic psychotherapist, efficacy is represented by the solution of the problem presented by the patient and the achievement of the objectives established at the beginning of the treatment.

Different theories of the human personality also provide for different objectives, and such differences also result in different evaluation methods.

Again, as Einstein believed, it is our perceptions and conceptions that determine our observations. In other words, it is our theoretical concept of human nature that determines our criteria for evaluating what is healthy or unhealthy, normal or pathological, and consequently also our concept of recovery and the objectives of therapy. For all these reasons, we have many different concepts of "recovery" and many different concepts of efficacy of treatment within the panorama of psychotherapy.

However, as Sirigatti (1988) reports, "At present there seems to be a certain agreement in defining a treatment to be efficacious when it leads to (a) symptom improvement, (b) increased ability to work, (c) better sexual adjustment, (d) improvement in interpersonal relations, (e) increased ability to confront common psychological difficulties, (f) increased ability to react to daily stress" (p. 230).

The strategic approach to therapy, as we have illustrated in previous works (Nardone 1991, Nardone and Watzlawick 1993), is not concerned with a theory that can succinctly describe the concepts of normality and abnormality, nor with an all-embracing theory of human nature. Therefore, it is a "nonnormative" model. It is tied to the constructivist philosophy of knowledge that, based on the idea of the irreducibility of human nature and behavior to a single, comprehensive description and explanation, is concerned with the appropriate means of making the individual's relationship with reality more functional. From this theoretical perspective, the efficacy of therapy is represented by the resolution of the patient's specific problem.

The concept of recovery does not, therefore, entail an (improbable) complete absence of problems, but rather the overcoming of a specific problem experienced by the patient in a specific time frame and context of his or her life. The evaluation of the effects of strategic therapy can therefore be considered to be in agreement with the criteria listed above, with the caveat that no absolute generalization can be defined, and that success or the lack of it will be ascertained in relation to the initial therapeutic objectives. Accordingly, success will involve the solution of the patient's presenting problem and the achievement of goals that were agreed upon at the outset of therapy. The criteria for establishing efficacy used in this evaluative inquiry are defined below.

To evaluate the efficacy of the treatment, we used two sets of parameters. The first is the outcome of therapy. Were the goals that the patient and therapist agreed upon at the beginning of therapy achieved? Were the patient's problems resolved at the end of therapy? Was there a shift in the original symptom? The second is whether the outcome is sustained over time. Were the results of therapy maintained or was there a relapse? Have new problems replaced the original ones?

Three follow-up sessions were arranged at three months, six months, and one year after the end of treatment. The follow-up sessions were conducted as interviews with the patient and his or her family or partner; the structured interview regards the points mentioned by Sirigatti (1988) and the objectives agreed upon at the outset of therapy.

We consider a case resolved and the treatment completely successful only when, in addition to fulfilling the first set of parameters, the second set of parameters is also fulfilled, that is, when the disappearance of symptoms and problems at the end of therapy is maintained over time, without relapses or substitution of new symptoms for the original ones.

Besides, success or the lack of it can have many dimensions, and therefore it is important to consider not only the categories of resolved or unresolved cases, but also the categories relative to cases that are considerably improved or little improved, and it is also crucial to evaluate the possibility of deterioration following the end of therapy (Sirigatti 1988).

The evaluation of the effects of therapy is based on five categories of results:

> *Resolved cases:* complete resolution of the problem at the end of therapy and absence of relapses within one year. *Much-improved cases:* cases with complete remission of symptoms at the end of therapy, that have presented a decisive improvement of their situation at the follow-up sessions, but with sporadic and slight, easily controllable relapses. *Little-improved cases:* partial remission of symptoms at the end of therapy, with occasional crises and recurrence of symptoms reported at follow-up. However, such problems were generally described as being less serious that those before therapy. *Unchanged cases:* treatment accomplished no significant change in the patient's situation after ten sessions. In these

cases, treatment ended after the tenth session because there was reason to believe that continuation was not likely to produce change. *Worsened cases*: treatment led to a worsening of the patient's condition. [Nardone and Watzlawick 1993, p. 120]

Beyond defining and measuring efficacy, it is important to evaluate it in relation to the nature of the patient's problems. In other words, for a sound evaluation of the efficacy of a therapeutic model, we need to know which type of problems the model confronts with greater or lesser efficacy.

Toward that end, the data presented below are grouped into the categories described in the previous chapters. The evaluation of efficacy was, in addition to being applied to the entire sample, also differentiated with regard to the types of problems treated. This empirically based set of categories is, as we have already mentioned, in keeping with the *DSM-IV* classifications of psychological and psychiatric diagnostic standards for all the presented disorders.

Purely experimental researchers might advance some doubts in relation to the criteria we have used to measure the efficacy of our therapeutic intervention. The criticisms that might be presented in relation to the described methodology are (1) that the follow-up sessions were conducted not by researchers external to the clinic where the therapies were carried out, but by members of the staff, even if not by the therapist himself; and (2) that the evaluation of the efficacy was not carried out according to a rigorous experimental procedure with control groups and double-blind procedures.

However, experienced researchers know the difficulties involved in practicing strictly experimental measurements with control groups and double-blind procedures in a clinical context, because this often conflicts with questions of professional ethics and, above all, with patients' resistance to being subjected to experiments.

Finally, considering the fact that evaluative research in the field of applied psychotherapy has always faced a difficult problem with the right to privacy, we feel that the evaluative research presented here, even with its declared limitations, should be considered a reliable contribution. It should not be forgotten that our treatments of all cases have been video-recorded; this material is neither the fruit of the therapist's memories or fantasies nor the work of a movie director.

In addition to documenting the changes reported by the patients and their families, this videotaped evidence of our work has also allowed us to observe the efficacy of our sequence of treatments, that is, how, stage after stage, the set objectives were reached through preestablished therapeutic maneuvers.

DATA ON 152 TREATED CASES: OUTCOME OF THE INTERVENTION

Having explained our methodological premises and the epistemological criteria that guided our group, we can now discuss our research results.

As mentioned above, the data refer to the sample group of phobic-obsessive patients treated at the Centro di Terapia Strategica, as described in Chapter 1.

Table 4–1 shows the efficacy of our model both at a general level of phobic-obsessive syndromes and at a differential level by type of disorder. The results of the application of our model to a sample of 152 cases demonstrate the great efficacy of this intervention.

The general success rate seems decisively higher than the standards described in the research literature on the efficacy of different psychotherapeutic approaches (Andrews and Harvey 1981, Bergin and Strupp

TABLE 4–1. Efficacy of the Treatment

Type of problem	Resolved cases		Much-improved cases		Little-improved cases		Unchanged cases		Total cases
	n	%	n	%	n	%	n	%	n
Agoraphobia	24	86	3	11	1	4	–	–	28
Panic attacks with agoraphobia or vice versa	51	84	6	10	4	7	–	–	61
Panic attacks	9	64	–	–	3	21	2	14	14
Obsessive compulsions	24	77	–	–	4	13	3	10	31
Hypochondriac fixations	12	67	2	11	2	11	2	11	18
Total of cases	120	79	11	7	14	9	7	5	152

1972, Garfield 1981, Giles 1983, Luborsky et al. 1975, Sirigatti 1988, Strupp and Hadley 1979). The positive results of our treatment are 86 percent (79 percent cases resolved and 7 percent much improved) while the research literature estimates a variability of positive results of psychotherapies that goes from a minimum of 40 percent to a maximum of 70 percent of cases treated.

It should also be observed that in some of the specific types of disorders the therapeutic success of our model is even higher compared with the general success rate. Indeed, our success rate for agoraphobia and agoraphobia with panic attacks is 95 percent and 94 percent.

Another important observation regarding the efficacy of the treatment is that the results obtained at the end of treatment have been maintained over time. Indeed, the measurements carried out in the three follow-up sessions—three months, six months, and one year after the end of treatment—have shown a very low percentage of relapses. Finally, we found no evidence of shifts in the original symptoms.

On the basis of what the empirical data show, we can also maintain that our interventions have not been superficial or cosmetic therapies, but an effective resolution of the problems presented by the patient.

AN EVALUATION OF THE EFFECTIVENESS OF THERAPY

An evaluation of a therapy's effectiveness is the parameter that shows the real value of the model in operation.

In the field of psychotherapy, the evaluation of the effectiveness (or cost/benefit ratio) of the therapy is, unfortunately, one of the aspects that receives the least consideration and research (Garfield 1980). This lack of attention, which has been noticed by a few researchers, may even be due to a deliberate omission with the purpose of covering up the very poor results, in terms of therapeutic effectiveness, obtained by the great majority of psychotherapeutic approaches, which, on average, take several years and hundreds of sessions to obtain often rather meager results.

For example, the Menninger Foundation's research on the effectiveness of psychoanalysis (the famous Menninger Psychotherapy Research Project, which lasted eighteen years) found a median duration of treatment equal to 837 sessions, with only 40 percent positive results. There is quite a difference between resolving a phobia in three months and resolving it in seven to ten years. But strangely, as Garfield (1980) notes, what one might have supposed to be a fundamental rule of professional ethics for any type of therapeutic practice—that one should try to resolve the patient's problems and suffering as quickly as possible—has not received much consideration from psychotherapists. Garfield explains this apparently incomprehensible attitude by saying that psychotherapeutic thought has been dominated for decades by the idea that, to be effective, therapy must be prolonged, deep, and complex.

But this view has been decisively refuted by research on the comparative efficiency of psychotherapy. In fact, the data show clearly that there are no significant differences between results obtained in long-term therapy and those obtained in shorter therapy (Avnet 1965, Butcher and Koss 1978, Garfield et al. 1971, Gurman and Kniskern 1978, Harris et al. 1963, 1964, Luborsky et al. 1975, Muench 1965, Nardone 1991, Philips and Wiener 1966, Shlien 1957, Sirigatti 1988, Weakland et al. 1974). Some research even indicated shorter-term therapies as more efficacious.

Thus, having demonstrated the real efficacy of our therapeutic intervention, it becomes necessary to assess its efficiency, since that is what determines the value of the intervention in terms of applicability and ethical respect for the patient's personality. The moral duty of all therapists is to make their patients feel better as quickly as possible. In other words, the less time it takes to reach a certain result, the more valuable that result will be. The less time it takes for the treatment to obtain the effective and permanent solution of the problem presented by the patient, the more positive the cost/benefit ratio of the therapy will be.

Therapeutic effectiveness is measured by a very simple operation of calculating the ratio between the median duration and the efficacy of the treatment.

Table 4–2 shows the effectiveness of our model of therapy: in 87 percent of our cases, the duration of treatment was 20 sessions or less; 24 percent of the cases were treated in 10 sessions or less.

TABLE 4–2. Effectiveness on the Sample Element

Duration of treatment*	No. of patients	%
From 4 to 10 sessions	37	24
From 11 to 20 sessions	96	63
From 21 to 30 sessions	16	11
From 31 to 34 sessions	3	2

*Median duration: 14 sessions.

If we judge these data in relation to the complexity and rigidity of the phobic symptomatologies we dealt with, we can see how important the service offered to the patient was. In other words, when a patient with symptoms that often have prevented him for years from leading an autonomous life is liberated from that symptomatology within a few months (from a minimum of about one month to a maximum of eight, with an average of three to four months), that patient has received an important therapeutic service.

If we compare this with the time usually employed by traditional forms of psychotherapy to resolve these typologies of psychological disorders—their estimated average ranging from seven years of psychoanalytic therapy (Garfield 1980) to two years of cognitive-behaviorist therapy (Sirigatti 1988)[1]—it becomes even more evident how surprisingly effective the brief strategic therapeutic model is in quickly resolving the problems it was developed for.

The tangible and important difference between recovering in a few months and recovering in a few years is the difference in the patient's quality of life, which may remain problematic and painful for a longer time when it could have been free of such problems much sooner.

Unfortunately, and perhaps as an effect of often fascinating and "profound" theorizations, many psychotherapists forget that a therapist's primary duty is to be ethically respectful of the person who is seeking help and has the right to feel better as soon as possible. If, to reach this result, it becomes necessary to utilize manipulative strategies, as in many of the tactics described in this volume, we maintain that such tactics are most ethical and correct insofar as the goal is to help the patients solve their problems and improve their well-being as quickly as possible. Therefore, the "kind trick" is not a cynical instrument of torture, but a useful tactic for overcoming resistance to change and shortening the therapy in addition to making it efficacious.

---

1. Communication at the Enna International Congress of Cognitive Psychotherapy.

5

The Strategic Approach and Other Models of Psychotherapy

Psychopathology: when there is nothing wrong with somebody, the best cure is to name his ailment.

Karl Kraus

Most of my fears about physical illness are related to doctors and their treatments, not to disease in itself.

Guido Ceronetti

Bateson said that to explain is always to draw distinctions, but it is from the interactive playoff between differences that we get evolutions or refinements of practical-theoretical constructs.

Our aim in this chapter is to compare the characteristics of the practical-theoretical model described so far with the characteristics of other models of therapy that have been applied to phobic-obsessive problems.

As specialist readers have surely observed, at the level of general epistemological theory, the model proposed here has an evident constructivist matrix (Foerster 1973, Glaserfeld 1979), and the construction of our model is essentially cybernetic (Ashby 1956, Bateson 1967, 1972, Keeney 1985, Wiener 1975). At the level of interventions, these premises have led to a purely strategic structuring of our operations.

We take the definition of *strategic logic* from formal logic. By *strategic approach* we mean one where objectives are the basis for constructing operations, that is, an approach is called strategic when, for each problem under analysis, it devises appropriate techniques and maneuvers that make it possible to reach the objectives (the solution of the problem). We also believe this formulation to be in accordance with Neumann's definition, in his *Theory of Games* (1944), of strategy as the set of tactical and technical maneuvers for winning a game.

This logical-epistemological assumption is by itself sufficient to mark a difference between the present approach and traditional forms of psychotherapy. With our approach the therapy is adapted to the patient; it is not the patient who has to adjust to the particular model of psychotherapy that the therapist has embraced. However, this is not to favor any form of wild eclecticism, but rather to propose a theory in which method and rigorousness are based on flexibility and the ability to adapt to the specific characteristics of each problem faced. Therefore, the epistemological foundations of this model are its characteristic of distinction; their apparently abstract assumptions lead to consequential, tangible operative praxes that are substantially different from those of traditional psychotherapies.

Another theoretical and consequently practical assumption that makes the strategic approach different is its understanding of the formation/persistence and change/solution of problems, or the idea that human problems arise from ways of perceiving realities that lead the patients who have adopted them to consequent modalities of reaction and behavior. This assertion is directly derived from radical constructivist theories (Watzlawick 1984) defining every reality as the product of the perspective, the cognitive elaborations, and the type of language adopted by a subject to communicate that reality to self, others, and the world (Nardone and Watzlawick 1993).

The change and solution of personal and interpersonal human problems can, therefore, only be reached by way of a change in the perceptive and reactive modalities through which the patient experiences reality. If only the patient's behavioral reactions are modified, the change will be a superficial one, or what Watzlawick calls a "change 1." In other words, the change will not break the system but only partially modify its internal functioning in time and space. After some time, the system will naturally readopt its preexisting equilibrium, and the superficially modified problem will reappear.

Moreover, changing a patient's perceptive modalities involves not only the cognitive aspects of perception, but also, and mainly, the emotional ones. Therefore, a cognitive reframing of the patient's problematic ways of perceiving and reacting is not sufficient to produce this change. The reframing must also change emotions by having the patient live through alternative experiences that the therapeutic intervention provides the impulse for. This will produce a change in the functioning of the patient's entire system of perception and reaction. It is after this essential change that the patient acquires the ability to control and manage previously anxiety-laden and uncontrollable situations, also at a conscious cognitive level.

Consequently, we also believe that dysfunctional situations can only change effectively if the intervention succeeds in overcoming resistances to change that are typical of any system,[1] by producing tangible experiences of alternative perceptions of and reactions to the problematic reality.

As a practical consequence, we utilize ways of interacting that influence patients to have the kind of tangible perceptive-reactive experience that can lead to the qualitative leap necessary for producing changes in the patient's relationship with realities experienced as problematic. This type of therapeutic interaction is based on injunctions, "kind tricks," paradoxes, and behavioral traps. As shown in the previous chapters, such stratagems make it possible to lead our patients through alternative experiences of perception of and reaction to anxiety-laden realities without their complete awareness of what is happening.

A basic stratagem usually employed in the first therapeutic moves is to shift the patient's attention away from attempted solutions and toward other reactions, under therapeutic suggestion. After initially experiencing a tangible change in the symptomatology, either under suggestion or as the effect of a therapeutic "trap," patients realize that they have done something that would have seemed impossible before.

Thus, in brief strategic therapy we change the tangible reality of the patient's experience first; only after this has occurred do we go ahead and make the patient aware of it. We follow the ancient Oriental philosophy of winning by deceit: "To be effective, the stratagem cannot be revealed." The trick can only be disclosed after producing the effect for which it was employed.

---

1. From the theory of systems, we derive the construct that every system resists change to its balance even when this balance is dysfunctional.

If we compare this approach with the usual therapeutic procedures of traditional schools of psychotherapy, we will see that the order of objectives has been reversed. In fact, most psychotherapies set out from the premise that change will occur as an effect of the patient's gradual acquisition of consciousness of his problems and their causes (reaching so-called insight). In brief strategic therapy, insight comes after the change, not before. In other words, the theory of change in traditional therapies is based on the epistemological concept of linear causality and gradual, continuous change; in brief strategic therapy, it is based on the epistemological concept of circular causality and discontinuity of change.

It is due to these differences in epistemological assumptions that it seems necessary, from a traditional perspective, to make the patient conscious of the therapist's maneuvers toward change, while from the strategic and constructivist perspective this seems not only unnecessary but even counterproductive because it increases the system's resistance to change.

This epistemological and consequently practical difference distinguishes the strategic approach from all other forms of therapeutic intervention. Our practical-theoretical assumptions, extensively described above and in other publications (Nardone-Watzlawick 1993, Watzlawick et al. 1974), are derived directly from modern developments in epistemology and research in the physical and natural sciences applied to the field of clinical psychology and psychotherapy.

As we go into more specific detail in our comparison of therapeutic procedures practiced by different orientations, we will also see that strategic therapy and other forms of psychotherapy have some techniques in common. But the existing practical-theoretical differences also determine some differences within those techniques; the same technique is used with different objectives and within strategies that are alternatives to each other.

However, our intention here is to outline a constructive comparison between the different techniques, showing how we have sometimes drawn from other approaches at the level of techniques and procedures. This comparison between our model of therapy and the most important traditional forms of psychotherapy can proceed in pairs.

In historical order, our first comparison should deal with models of therapy that are based on intrapsychic factors and the constructs derived from psychoanalytic theories. We consider our model to be an alternative both in theory and practice to any form of psychoanalysis. Therefore, such a comparison, whose only result would be a negative examination of the typical theories and procedures of psychoanalytic approaches, would seem useless.

Behaviorism is the first approach with whose specific type of treatment we can make a comparison.

The contact points that can be observed between the brief strategic model of therapy and the behaviorist model for treating severe forms of fear lie in the use of rigorous models and some similar intervention techniques. The behaviorist approach was surely the first to develop specific forms of treatment for phobic disorders (Bandura 1974, 1977, Skinner 1974, Wolpe 1958, 1973). Behaviorist scholars and therapists were also the first to pay due attention to the problem of evaluating the efficacy of their therapeutic interventions. As for techniques, some behaviorist techniques have been reelaborated and adapted to our model of brief therapy for phobic problems. They are (1) symptom monitoring, which we, however, employ in a suggestive-injunctive form; and (2) gradual desensitization *in vivo*, although in our case this is joined with techniques of hypnosis without trance.

Other techniques presently used in strategic therapy can be regarded as evolutions of behaviorist intervention techniques, with the practical difference that we utilize personal influence and suggestive-hypnotic types of communication that the emphatically aseptic behaviorist approach will not consider (Sirigatti 1975).

As already mentioned, however, the greatest difference at the applied level is that behaviorist interventions focus on reducing and controlling the patient's responses to menacing realities, while strategic interventions focus on changing ways of perceiving menacing realities and consequently changing the phobic patient's behavioral responses. In one case, therefore, we have a superficial intervention on reactions; in the other, we have a deep intervention that not only changes reactions, but also the perceptions of the realities that initiated the phobic reactions.

The third, and historically very relevant, model of psychotherapy with which a comparison can be made is client-centered therapy (Rogers 1954). Although Rogerian therapists have not developed any form of intervention specifically for phobic-obsessive disorders, a common trait, as with the behaviorists, is attention to method in our interventions and to the evaluation of results. Another important observation is that, while employing different techniques, both client-centered and brief strategic therapists make great effort to put the patient in a state of empathy and willingness to collaborate in the therapy. Empathy and collaboration are produced, in the first case, by Rogerian mirroring techniques and in the second by the technique of suggestive hypnotic tracing of the patient's communicative styles. We might say with an amusing paraphrase that Rogerian therapy is client-centered, while strategic therapy is therapist-centered, because the Rogerian mirrors the client and tries to avoid any direct influence, while the strategist uses the patient's own language and perceptive-reactive modalities to deliberately influence the patient to change.

If we were to follow a strict chronological order in our exposition of methodological comparisons, we would now discuss the contributions of Milton Erickson's hypnotic approach to psychotherapy and its derivations. But since the Ericksonian methodologies and therapeutic style were the first expression of strategic therapy, such a reference would seem redundant.[2]

However, a theoretical and methodological comparison between the strategic approach described here and the various orientations of the systemic view of psychotherapy seems necessary. First of all, we need to consider that the strategic approach to therapy is an integrated evolution of the systemic approach to therapy that was founded by the renowned Palo Alto group (Don D. Jackson, J. Haley, V. Satir, J. Weakland, and P. Watzlawick). The first systemic-strategic formulations of that group of therapist-researchers later divided into two main branches of strategic therapy: the brief therapy of the Mental Research Institute in Palo Alto (Watzlawick et al. 1974) and the approach developed by J. Haley at the Washington Institute, with the contribution of Montalvo, Minuchin, and Madanes (Madanes 1981). Through his work at the Milwaukee Brief Family Therapy Center a decade later, de Shazer (1994) further developed previous formulations of brief therapy, based on the systemic perspective, into a "solution-oriented" model of treatment.

The model of brief strategic therapy that has emerged from our research-intervention on phobic-obsessive patients is a further evolution of these strategic models, particularly in its development of strategic intervention plans for specific problems (Nardone 1991, Nardone and Watzlawick 1993). Thus, the *systemic matrix* of our model is clearly recognizable if we let that term refer exclusively to the model of systemic therapy that was born and developed at the Mental Research Institute in Palo Alto (and from our perspective, it would not be wrong to define it thus). But if the systemic approach is taken to mean a broader viewpoint that includes all

---

2. The evolution of the systemic approach, from its first Ericksonian expressions to the formulations of models of brief strategic therapy in the 1970s, and up to the present formulations of brief strategic and constructivist therapy, has been extensively discussed in other works (Nardone 1991, Nardone and Watzlawick 1993).

orientations of family therapy in its mainstream, as the voluminous literature on this subject would seem to imply, then an explanation of the theoretical and practical differences between those models and ours is necessary.

A first difference, not merely a practical one but one arising from a clearly defined theoretical viewpoint, is that the systemic-familiarist tradition has a "relational prejudice," as the authors themselves define it (Cecchin 1990). It sees the relationship between members of a family as the main cause of problem persistence; therefore, it is always considered necessary to include the family in the therapeutic setting. From our strategic-constructivist point of view, as we have explained many times before, problem persistence derives from a patient's perceptions and perspective on the reality that forces him or her to have the so-called dysfunctional behavioral reactions toward this reality—these reactions being attempted solutions to the problem. We also believe that the relational typologies or, as we prefer to define them, the typologies of interaction between the patient and reality, cannot be limited to the interaction between the patient and other people but is more correctly represented as a complex system of interdependence between the patient's relations with self, others, and the world (Figure 5–1).

If, within this interdependent system of interactions, even just one of the three typologies works dysfunctionally, the whole system will become invalid. Thus, with respect to the typical theoretical tradition of approaches to family therapy, we introduce the additional factor of the relationship between the mind and the mind. Thus we introduce within the systemic relational model, which in its opposition to psychodynamic intrapsychic models avoided considering intrapsychic dynamics, a constructivist and cognitive model that can no longer be ignored in view of the evolutions of basic psychological research and the most recent epistemological formulations.

In strictly practical terms, applied to a human system that is going through a crisis, the model of an interdependent system of relationships

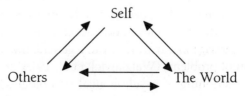

FIGURE 5–1. The complex system of interdependence

(Figure 5–1) makes it possible to see which of the three relational typologies can be used as the main lever of intervention, in order to set a quick and effective change in motion within that system. In the case of the phobic-obsessive disorders examined by us, it became clear that the most advantageous focus of the therapeutic intervention was on the relationship between the patient and self. As our case examples and the different models of intervention for the different types of disorders we analyzed show in more detail, changes in the relationship with other people and the world occur because of changes introduced, by particular therapeutic stratagems, within the patient's relationship with the self.

Thus, one considerable difference between our model and models of family therapy lies in the use of different kinds of settings for therapy. In our model, the setting can be individual, couple, family, or a mixed group, according to the needs of the case; we adapt the therapy to the problem and not the problem to the model of therapy.

In the specific case of phobic-obsessive disorders, our research-intervention has led to the development of an individual treatment protocol that is only indirectly systemic.

Another practical and theoretical difference between our model of strategic constructivistic therapy and models of family therapy lies in our deliberate use of suggestion and injunctive communication derived from the tradition of studies on hypnosis. Most current approaches to family therapy (Andolfi 1991, Cancrini 1987, Selvini-Palazzoli et al. 1989) show a strong psychoanalytic matrix that reintroduces the epistemological and practical limitations inherent in models based on the concept of linear causality.

What distinguishes our model of brief strategic therapy from the Mental Research Institute's model is that, from the very beginning, our adaptation to the Italian cultural context of techniques developed for the American cultural context led to considerable transformations in the clinical application of many therapeutic procedures. Thus we find a first observable difference at the level of communication and interaction with the patient, due to the existence of significant cultural differences between the two contexts. A second difference lies in our research and systematic preparation of specific protocols for specific psychological symptomatologics. At the practical and theoretical level, this development has led to an even more productive passage in our work, from a general theory on the formation and solution of problems (Watzlawick et al. 1974) to specific formulations on the functioning of psychological pathologies and their rapid solution. In relation to the original practical and theoretical formulations of the Palo Alto group, the present work, like previous work by our group, thus represents an evolution in the direction of the specific study of systems of psychological problems and their solution through replicably effective strategies.

The last comparison that remains to be made between our model and the other contemporary forms of psychotherapy is with cognitive psychotherapy. Like the systemic approach, cognitive psychotherapy includes many different orientations within the same theoretical mainstream: from constructivists (Kelly 1955) to evolutionists in the style of Mahoney (1979), to Ellis's (1978) rational-emotional therapies, to the cognitive-behavioral psychotherapy of Beck and Emery (1985), to cognitivist authors who have reintroduced psychodynamic concepts and formulations.

It is clearly important, in fact necessary, to make a methodological comparison of our approach and those cognitive approaches that aim for a swift extinction of the symptomatology and a cognitive reframing of the patient's personality. However, it would be useless to propose a comparison between a model of brief therapy oriented toward the rapid and effective solution of problems, such as ours is, and those orientations of cognitive psychotherapy that, by reintroducing psychodynamic concepts, also reintroduce an indifference to the effectiveness of their intervention on the patient's cruel symptomatology in order to privilege a slow and gradual cognitive reframing.

As we mentioned in Chapter 3, we tested some cognitive-behavioral techniques of intervention on phobias as we were developing our own model. At the strategic level, one basic difference between a focused brief therapy approach and a cognitive therapy approach is the almost complete inversion of the intervention process.

According to the cognitive orientation, the change and solution of a problem are reached through the patient's gradual learning of new cognitive schemes. Such learning is necessarily acquired through conscious processes. However, our point of view is that one first produces concrete changes in the patient's experiences of frightening situations through stratagems, kind tricks, and so on. Having produced such a change, one proceeds toward a cognitive reframing by which the patient acquires new perceptive, cognitive, and behavioral modalities with respect to the problem. While the cognitivist resolves the problem of fear, panic, and phobia through a gradual change in the patient's cognition, the strategist resolves the same problem by using techniques that find their way around the patient's resistance to change and present experiences of new and concrete ways of perceiving and relating to fear.

Even though the epistemological theory of reference (constructivism, the complexity of the mind, circular causality) and many therapeutic techniques (reframing, prescriptions, and so on) at times make the two models look very similar, in clinical practice they are clearly very different.

Moreover, the communication style of strategic therapists aims to exercise a marked and deliberate personal influence on the patient and utilizes hypnotic language and injunctive procedures, while the communication style of cognitive therapists aims to produce a change in the patient's cognition and consciousness and is therefore based on a language of reason and conscience. In other words, in brief strategic therapy the style of communication is injunctive (Austin 1962, Brown 1973), suggestive, and performative, while the cognitive style of communication is indicative, prescriptive, and explanatory.

To conclude this chapter, we want to emphasize, as has been made clear by the methodological and procedural comparisons we have just presented, that our model is based on a theoretical pluralism and cognitive pragmatism (Salvini 1988) that make it flexible and adaptable without letting it fall into any form of inconsistent eclecticism or rigid technicalism. In cybernetic terms, our model can be represented as an open system, based on the interdependent interaction between theory and practical application, within which the principle of self-correction, based on the effects of our interventions, is considered.

Part II

Case Examples

To be worthy, and be able to show it, is to be twice worthy; if something cannot be seen, it is as if it were not there.

Baldasar Gracian

Presenting a transcript of a therapeutic interaction, punctuated in all its moves and countermoves, seems the best way to enable readers to enter into the spirit of a process of change such as brief therapy, even at the risk of making our exposition seem tedious.[1] But considering the typology of these cases and treatments, we believe that, on the contrary, this record will be readable and even interesting. The two clinical cases that follow in Chapters 6 and 7 are examples of treatments that include creative therapeutic maneuvers.

---

1. This full transcript of the therapies (omitting names and places in order to guarantee patient anonymity; however, we have their permission to publish their treatment) and identification of moves was carried out by a group of students and collaborators. The author is grateful to Angelita Malfetti, Costantino Casilli, Rita Rocchi, Manuela Giannotti, Branka Skorjanec, Leonardo Bruni, and Aldo Chiappini, as well as Laura Del Citerna who has reviewed their work together with me.

We want to show that the resolution of complicated and painful problems does not necessarily have to be just as painful and complicated; it can be a kind of interactive game between the therapist and the patient. The difficulty lies in the fact that it is easy to complicate things, but difficult to make them simple.

6

How to Rupture the Fear of Fear: A Case of Agoraphobia with Panic Attacks

FIRST SESSION

The patient is a 37-year-old woman, married with a child, and holds a Ph.D. in political science.

Defining the Problem and Inquiring about Attempted Solutions

T. Well, what is the problem?

P. It's quite difficult to . . . no, maybe it isn't so difficult . . . but let me start from the beginning. I began quite suddenly to feel ill, as I remember it, although if I think about it, there had been some slight signs of warning three years ago, when I suddenly started having strange spells of dizziness. That's what I called them then, anyway, although it was quite a different matter on the whole. And . . . there had been some previous related occurrences. I think I had a congestion one day. That sort of thing. When I fell sick, I stayed home for quite a long time—about fifteen days. My blood pressure was eighty, so the doctor said it was a matter of stress. Actually, my blood pressure used to drop steeply . . . that kind of thing. After some time . . . immediately, in fact, I went to see a doctor, had some checkups and an electrocardiogram. I felt reassured and very calm, because everything seemed to be all right. The summer went by . . . the holidays went well. Around September I started going to a center in Florence once every three weeks . . . they prescribed sessions. At first they made me take some medicines. . .

T.   Is that the psychoanalyst . . .

P.   It's in the same center, but I initially went to this Doctor S., where I didn't actually do analysis . . . at least I don't think so . . . anyhow, that subject was so distant from me, so distant . . . I'm the kind of person to whom you would never, ever expect this sort of thing to happen. I've always been an extremely rational and rationalizing person. There was no reason to get sick; one just didn't get sick.

T.   Good. First Doctor S., and medicines and meetings.

P.   Yes, medicines and meetings. I started with Laroxil and Xanax, not in strong doses.

T.   For how long?

P.   More or less until the spring. Then they told me to stop taking the Laroxil. I have continued to take one Xanax a day.

T.   Then you began psychoanalysis. . . .

P.   Yes, around September the same year. We had talked before about a need to examine the whole situation. I asked him . . . I had learned a lot during that time; I had gotten over a lot of things. That is to say, I had gotten over all the purely physical complaints, and those complaints that could be related to something physical—overcome them completely. So much so that I have high blood pressure now—good blood pressure.

There's nothing wrong with me anymore, let's put it that way.

T. That was with Doctor S., who is a psychiatrist.

P. Yes. At that point, I asked him what use it was to me, if it didn't help me feel completely well. I don't mean to feel like before. When I first went there, I wanted to feel like I did before, but later I discovered that maybe it wasn't right, apart from the fact that it probably wasn't even possible. . . . But there were probably some reasons why I had gotten sick, so. . . . But to feel at least as well as I did before. . . . In the meantime, everything related to physical complaints has gone away. All that's left is a sense of . . . "being lost," as I call it, which is very strong when it seizes me, and prevents me from feeling capable of dealing. . . .

Anticipation Technique   T. What exactly do you feel: vertigo, breathing difficulties, accelerated heartbeat, trembling . . . ?

P. [interrupting] Occasionally, accelerated heartbeat. Only occasionally. . . . Not breathing difficulties; mainly accelerated heartbeat. Not always. I would say that I feel "outside the world," unable to perceive the whole reality. Seeing things . . .

T. Out of focus.

P. Out of focus. Almost.

T. Are your eyes unfocused or is it that your mind is confused ?

P. Let's say that things in my mind are not as well defined as they are when I look at them when I feel well, and that happens . . . a lot. My main reaction is that I don't feel like going out anymore, in the sense that I'm afraid of finding myself in that kind of situation, because it's beyond my control. As long as I had low blood pressure, I used to take my drops along; that was an excuse. Now, knowing that there is nothing physically wrong with me, I am completely unable to . . . and if I try to rationalize . . . like some people say, who tell me to "make an effort." I believe they say that because they've never tried to realize that the moment one tries to make an effort is exactly the moment when one can't make it.

Use of Metaphor
and "Mirroring"
Technique

T.   It's like putting a cat in a bag: the more you push it, the angrier it gets, and it scratches, and breaks the bag. . . . Once the cat is out, it becomes even angrier. The cat needs to be educated.

P.   Yes, that's true. And while I have been able to overcome everything that had to do with something I knew . . . at this point, I don't see any solution. The strange thing is that I never used to be afraid before. I mean, I know people who are unwell, or not very well, who believe that they have some serious illness whenever they're not feeling well. I have never had any fears of that kind, because I have always been able to . . . , well, with more or less serious physical problems. It's this . . . , so . . . , thing. It's no accident that this has hit me in what I used to be best at: my self-control.

T.   So now, if I've understood you right, you avoid going out alone.

P.   [interposing] Yes . . . I'm very much afraid of that.

T.   You avoid being alone. . . .

P.   No, not being alone. . . . Enclosed places are all right for me—at least, familiar places are fine with me: my home, my friends' homes, going to the theater. Oddly enough, I never have any problems at the theater.

T.   Why, should you?

P.   No, actually not. When I'm at the theater, I'm doing something specific. If I have to do the shopping, that in itself creates . . . I know that I might feel ill, and when that happens I feel so bad that it even bothers me to think about having to do it.

Inquiring about
Attempted Solutions

T. So do you ask for help and support from the people around you?

P. Now I do; it's taken me almost three years to get to that point.

T. Of asking for help?

P. I wasn't in the habit of asking for help; on the contrary, I was probably a person who didn't ask for very much help from other people. I mean . . .

T. Why did you answer: "It's taken me three years (of analysis) to . . ."?

P. [interrupting] I think . . .

T. Is it a great success for you to be able to ask for help?

P. No, it's no great success. It is still difficult for me to admit that I need help, but before I just didn't admit it. I used to find an excuse first: "I've got a headache. . . ." At this point, I believe that I needed the physical signs of illness to be able to accept that I was unhappy. For example, if somebody had told me four years ago that something like this would happen to me, I would have said it was absolutely impossible. When I happen to talk about this, to give an example, I say: "When I gave birth to my child and had to have a cesarean, I was calmer than everyone else; it was I who gave courage to the others. I mean, there they stood, looking at my belly . . ."

T. You are married, with one child?

P. Yes.

T. How old is the child?

P. Eight.

T. What do you do in your life?

P. I work for the public administration in B. I live in B. and work in B.

T. And what does your husband do?

P.   He works at the Mountain Community. [she laughs] We are two frustrated public employees.

T.   So you initially turned to Doctor S., and then you started analysis. Who are you doing analysis with?

P.   The name is . . .

T.   Is it a woman?

P.   Yes, she's a woman, but I can't remember her name.

T.   How often do you go to analysis?

P.   Three times a week.

T.   Freudian therapy?

P.   I don't know anything about that. It's so difficult.

T.   How long have you been doing that?

P.   For three years, apart from a couple of sessions earlier. . . . I used to say that I was simply going there as a necessary evil, let's put it that way, in order to get well. Now, after three years, something about all that is starting to interest me. Aside from the fact that for the moment I certainly don't feel any better; on the contrary, I sometimes think I've gotten worse . . . still . . .

T.   What does the psychoanalyst trace your fears to?

P.   She and I talk a lot about a child-part that needs to come out. . . . I don't know. I am actually discovering . . . I mean when . . . before I got ill, I think I had gotten to the point of . . . softening every blow, not having any reactions . . . of being controlled from the outside to such a degree that I had become controlled from the inside too. I have rediscovered some very strong feelings since then. The first, immediate one was . . . anger, I would say. I mean, I realized that I had spent some time accepting everything that happened to me, even convincing myself that I was happy about it, that I had made the best choices, that. . . . Later I discovered that they may have been the most logical ones, but it was also correct to say that I had done some things . . . chosen the best solution, perhaps, but I was missing out on some things. I admit that I missed some things. In particular, I was then thinking about the subject of work; I mean, one studies for a degree, graduates in political science with good grades. One has good possibilities. Then logically one chooses. Among other things, I was already married and had a child when I got my degree, and choosing (rightly, too; I would probably make the same choice again; I would still do it) to try for a job at the public administration in B., where you do everything except what you might apply a major in economics to; it's like putting it away on a shelf. But maybe at the time my reaction was to convince myself that it was good, it was nice, without accepting the fact that I missed certain things, like the possibility of . . . I mean, I could have gone to the graduate school in Turin if I hadn't been married. If I hadn't had a child, I would probably have gone anyway; then, I mean. . . .

Reframing through
Metaphor

T.   Where I come from, people used to say, "If my grandmother had had wheels, she would have been a cart, but my grandmother was sorry she wasn't a cart, although . . .

P.   Yes, that's the idea. Anyway, this is probably . . . still . . . that is, it's still a valid solution. Why shouldn't I say that I miss having the time to read like when I was a student? I mean, it's much more honest to say that I miss my studies very much because I have to run around among administrative resolutions and telephone calls which I don't give a damn about.

T.   All right. With that, we are entering a context that I believe to be secondary. What we have in the forefront is the problem that brings you here. If I've understood you correctly, it's these no-better-identified crises of panic, anxiety, phobia, or I'm not sure what, and the anger that comes with them. There's one thing I am curious about: Has the analyst been told that you have turned to me?

P. No.

T. Well, do you want to go ahead with both treatments at the same time? Did you come here out of curiosity? What's the attitude?

P. I came here because although I expect to get something out of the analysis, I realize that it's not a very speedy matter, and I can't stand it. I mean, I would like to . . . there are some things about this matter that interest me. I feel that I am experiencing . . . I am attempting to bring out something that . . . that I didn't know before. And yet, I feel very disoriented, because of what use is all this to me when I still need someone to accompany me, someone who . . . by doing that, among other things . . . I don't know how to say this, but . . . I feel the weight of the people around me. And I feel it . . .

T. And you feel it even more this way, because you need it.

P. Of course.

T. It's very simple.

P. In the beginning, I thought I would do analysis in order to feel well again. A few days ago, I thought that I would like to get well because then I'd be free to do analysis, and not depend on those who one may or may not care . . .

T. I think your analyst has been very good. [smiles]

P. And anyhow, my priority is to get well. I don't know. When I get well, I probably won't care the least about doing analysis; maybe that's what will happen. I don't have the faintest idea; I just imagine that's how it will be. But I have discovered in the past three years that I don't know very much about myself in that sense; now and again, something happens which makes it seem that I always have to start from the beginning again, and this inability to define. . . . It used to feel so good, although it probably isn't true that it used to feel so good, but it used to feel so good when I still had all my certainties. . . .

Reframing by Using a Metaphor

T. You know, I always say that sometimes, when we enter certain kinds of circuits, we are the centipede who could walk perfectly well, uphill and downhill, climbing trees, doing extreme evolutions of movements, and who one day had to answer a very embarrassing question from an ant who asked, "But can you explain how you are able to walk so well with a hundred feet at the same time?" The centipede started to think about how difficult it was to walk with a hundred feet at the same time [pause] and was no longer able to walk.

P. I agree, that's what it's like. Yes, yes, certainly.

Agreeing on the Modalities of the Treatment

T. First of all, I must explain my method in the sense that you are used to a kind of approach that I believe is many miles distant from my personal approach.

P. But which still disconcerts me, you know.

Therapeutic Double Bind

T. I am a decidedly pragmatic person. My way of working is very pragmatic; I do very brief therapies. I allow myself ten sessions: if the problem is resolved within ten sessions, well and and good. If I have produced some significant changes within ten sessions, but we have not yet reached the desired result, then we can continue. If I have not changed anything within ten sessions, from my point of view this means that I wouldn't be able to change anything in a hundred seasons; I discontinue the treatment. [pause] My methods are a bit peculiar, because apart from talking, which is an important aspect but not the most important one, I make people do many things, I ask them to do many things. But the nicest thing about that is that, more often than not, the things I ask people to do are apparently illogical, rather strange things which may seem banal at times, and which must be carried out without asking any questions. Explanations are provided, but later. All right? So those are the rules of my way of working. All right?

P.   Yes.

T.   So if you agree, I will already start giving you some tasks to perform. I think it is also necessary to do something (concretely), to act concretely, especially with these kinds of problems.

P.   What about the fact that I have these strange commitments?

T.   Your sessions with the analyst?

P.   Is that a problem for you?

T.   You see, I always say that I don't have any counter-recommendations—none at all. I am open and accessible; I believe it will be the analyst who will give you some problems.

P.   Meaning what?

T.   Well, psychoanalysts define me as a heretic, so I expect that there will be some resistances, as they say in jargon.

P.   Yes, yes, yes. No, that's all right. But I've told you that it represented something new to me, something new that, among other things, is very difficult for me to . . .

T.   Good, good. I would like to proceed with the first reflection that I invite you to make during the coming week. Every time that you ask for help and receive it, I would like you to think that you are simultaneously receiving two messages: one, evidently, is "I care about you; I help and protect you." The second, less evident, but subtler and stronger, is "I help you because you can't make it alone; because you are sick when left to yourself."

Reframing by Inducing the "Fear of Help"

T.   In the long run, the second of these messages not only contributes to the persistence of your symptoms of fear, but also makes them more severe. Because this confirmation really functions as a reinforcement and an incentive to your symptomatology. But please note that I am not asking you to stop asking for help, because you are not yet capable of doing without help. I am only asking you to think that every time you ask for help and receive it, you contribute to the persistence and aggravation of your problems. But, please, do not make any efforts to succeed in not asking for help, because you are not capable of not asking for help. Only think that each time you ask for it and receive it, you contribute to making things worse.

First Prescription: "Log"   T. [prosodic pause] Moreover, I will give you another task, for a start; here it is. I have prepared a simple form that you will reproduce on every page of a pocket-size notebook. You must fill in the date, the time, the place, and the people present; situations, thoughts, symptoms, reactions. Every time, from now until next week, that you have one of your attacks, you will immediately write down briefly in the notebook, wherever you are, whoever is with you: the date, place, people present, context, thoughts, symptoms, and the reactions that come to you. All right? It is important that you do it at that very moment. Even if the same thing happens a hundred times the same day, you will write the same thing a hundred times, because I need to be well informed on both the frequency and the intensity; I must have a precise set of data on what is happening. Good. And this task must remain a secret between us. You can tell your husband that "they are giving me homework," but you mustn't tell him what it is. This is true for all prescriptions that I will give you, and there will be many of them.

P.   And what if I avoid situations and dangers?

T.   We shall see.

SECOND SESSION

The woman came back reporting only two episodes on the log, but explained that usually she avoided all situations that seemed dangerous for her. It was thus necessary to insist on redefining the attempted solutions of "seeking help" and "controlling the fear at a rational level" through explanations and metaphors. Then I repeated the reframing of the "fear of help," and added a redefinition of the attempted solution of avoidance.

> T.   So you have become very good at avoiding.
> P.   Oh, very good.
> T.   It's the technique of avoidance, as I call it; it's one of those attempted solutions that complicate the problem, because "since I've always avoided this one, I'm going to avoid this other one, then this other one, then this other one, then this other one, then this other one, until one . . .

The session proceeded along very philosophical lucubrations (following the patient's language and logic) until the final phase of prescriptions:

The Log Prescription is Maintained

> T.   Well, well. Let's go on to my nice little tasks. I am going away for two weeks, as I think you already know. But I will give you homework for the whole period. The tasks are exactly the following: first of all you have to continue doing this one [pointing to the log]; you must think that every time you ask for help, you contribute to worsening your symptoms. Moreover, you should start thinking that every time you avoid something, you contribute even more to aggravating your symptoms. So every time you ask for help and receive it, you aggravate your symptoms; every time you avoid doing something, even the smallest thing . . .

Redefinition: "Avoid Avoiding"

> P.   I have to plunge into it.
> T.   I usually say, if you really must avoid something, then avoid avoiding. All right?
> P.   I understand. Now I'll have to start going shopping again.

Prescription:
Paradoxical Ritual of
Worst Fantasy
Technique for Half an
Hour a Day

T. Avoid avoiding. Moreover, every day over the next fifteen days, at a time that we'll decide upon, I want you to take an alarm clock. Have you got an alarm clock?

P. Yes, yes.

T. Good. You take your alarm clock, lock yourself into a room where you can be alone, set the alarm to sound after half an hour, draw the curtains or the blinds, make yourself comfortable, and try to imagine all the greatest dangers, all the worst situations in which you might feel terror, fear. You must make a voluntary effort to feel as bad is you can, provoking your own anxiety crises by imagining panic-laden situations; and do anything that comes to your mind: if you feel like crying, cry; if you feel like tearing your hair, tear your hair; if you feel like screaming, scream; if you feel like rolling on the floor, roll on the floor. Where the alarm sounds, you turn it off, and it's all over. You go and wash your face, and return to your usual day.

P. Subjective panic? . . . I mean, shall I think of situations in which I might really find myself, or tragic situations?

T. Even the most tragic ones; the more tragic, the better. The worse you manage to feel, the better.

P. I'm not able to. . . .

T. Perfect. Then you will tell me what happened. Every day. At what time can we do it ?

P. At what time can we do it . . . not in the morning, because I'm at work until two.

T. Well, around three o'clock. All right?

P. Around three o'clock.

T. From three to three-thirty every day. All right?

THIRD SESSION

Reframing the Effect
of the First
Prescription

T. So, how was your week?

P. I don't know. I had a fairly good week, in some respects; in fact I did not have many moments of crisis.

T. Good.

P. Also because . . .

T. You have only recorded two episodes.

P. And the second episode was only a beginning; I went through a couple more situations that stopped at the beginning stage. In general, I wrote this in the log, too, I started talking at some point and that resolved it. It was always . . . at the beginning, the situation was . . . I tried to avoid avoiding, and so . . . I don't mean to say that now I'm a lion who can do anything. On the whole, there's a little . . . in the background, but there's no longer . . .

T. There's no longer?

P. There's no longer a situation . . . that is, apart from the situations that I've mentioned, . . . a situation in which I was quite . . . a strong situation, let's say.

Positive Reinforcement on the Possibility of Reducing the Symptoms

T. So we can say that in the course of about two weeks, there have been only two episodes, one of which was rather bland.

P. Yes.

T. Can we call that a considerable improvement or not?

P. I don't know. In some respects . . .

T. A considerable improvement with respect to the symptoms, their frequency, and their intensity . . . How much shall we give it in percentage? What grade shall we give it in percentage?

P. Surely 50 percent. The remaining 50 percent is a condition of not feeling perfectly secure, not completely calm about making decisions.

She also declared that she had not taken any pills, that she had never considered doing it, and that she had stopped using the attempted solutions of "avoidance."

P. I have not found myself back in a situation where. . . . In short, I have avoided avoiding.

T.   What does "I have avoided avoiding" mean? That you didn't shrink away from anything at all?

P.   It means that when I realized it, that is, as I have told you, I used to be much more depressed; I mean, if I didn't feel up to going out, that was fine: I used to find an excuse not to go. To give you an example, here's the second episode, which was over soon after it began: That morning, at work, I was supposed to go to the bank and cash a check. There had been a few similar situations before, when I had appealed to my colleagues. "Are you by any chance going out? Are you going to the bank, by any chance?" I was about to do that again, but then I told myself, "No, I've got to go; let's see what happens." So I avoided avoiding in that sense. I think . . . I mean, I still haven't . . . I don't go searching for more opportunities than I have to. I mean, I don't say, "Well, I've got nothing to do today; let me think up something to do for myself." But whenever it was necessary, I simply went, without looking for somebody to ask "Are you by any chance going that way and could you please fetch me . . . if not, I'll go myself, but if you would be so kind . . ." I did what I had to, and that was that.

T.   Good.

The session continued with a redefinition of the change that had occurred, and then with patient's report on the second prescription.

Redefining the Second Prescription

T.   Well, what happened during the famous half-hour?

P.   A whole set of problems came up.

T.   Oh. Let's talk about it.

P.   Let's talk about the problems. First problem: the first day, I did everything I could to forget, and didn't remember until the evening. At that point I faced an enormous problem, because you had said that I was always supposed to do it at the same time of day, so naturally I felt lost. I said to myself: "What do I do now? Shall I start tomorrow, or shall I do it at eight in the evening, or shall I call him and ask?" Then I found my own personal solution, continuing to do it at the same time in the evenings, but I don't know whether that was the right thing to do. So that was the first problem, which, however, I resolved the first day; I made a decision that I had to make anyhow. It all went quite peacefully until about two days ago. . . .

T. Well, the important thing was to do it at the same time every day. Very good.

P. Then there was another kind of problem. I believe there's some attempt to avoid here, too, because I tried to think about things that make me anxious and, to be honest, the things that came to my mind were not anxiety provoking at all; I mean, they were only slightly anxiety provoking. I mean, I identified one thing that I thought would surely make me anxious in the idea that something might happen to N., and told myself, "Well, if I think about something like that, it will certainly make me feel awful." The first day, I imagined things like "he bruises his leg." "No, I've got to think of something worse." I mean, there was clearly an attempt to stop the process.

At this point, I proceeded to redefine the stratagems I had used.

Reframing the Two Strategies Employed as New Ways to Deal with Fears

T. Well, I believe that I should give you some explanation for these strange things, shouldn't I? Basically the half-hour and the log have two aims—they are two strategies for reaching specific aims. First of all, the log is not just a collection of data; it is what we call a "symptom-shifting technique," meaning that the act of writing down something very embarrassing immediately shifts the attention away from listening to oneself, and toward the task to be performed; thus, we obtain a reduction of the symptoms. That's one specific stratagem. The half-hour has a different function that is even more peculiar, because here we employ para-doxical logic, in the idea that *similia similibus curantur*. Instead of trying to stop something, or to repress it, we deliberately provoke and exas-perate it. We know that if we do that certain symptoms will disappear, because when a symp-tom becomes voluntary it's not a symptom any-more; to remain a symptom it has to be com-pulsive, involuntary, something that comes by itself. Thus, the two little games that I have played with you are two little games, two strata-gems to break the symptomatic rigidity, to break the perceptive-reactive system that was forcing you to have certain responses.

P.   Yesterday I asked myself how come I was think-ing about all the work I had to do while going to bed one evening. I had a lot to do at work and was behind schedule.

The focus was on enabling the patient to feel self-confident in using the new strategy to deal with symptoms.

T.   From now on, you can use those strategies delib-erately, as you progressively expose yourself to situations that have, until now, been too anxiety-laden for you, as you have already done by going to the bank, by going out to do other things. Without knowing it, you were using and profit-ing from what I had provoked. And you must continue to do so. Then it will be good to con-tinue in the same direction. So: avoid avoiding; quickly and promptly exasperate the situation whenever there's a crisis; use the log, but only if you need to; the half hour is not important anymore, because you must do it all the time. All right? I'll see you again next week. Now, every time you happen to feel scared, you must promptly exasperate the whole thing. Avoid avoiding, also because I'm giving you another week; after that, I will start asking you to do a few things for me. All right?

FOURTH SESSION

The session started, as usual, with an evaluation of the events of the previous week.

Redefining the Effect of the Prescription and the Changes

T.   So, what happened in the past week?

P.   It was pretty quiet, not particularly stressful; in fact, I didn't have any great. . . . I mean, I haven't got any notes to show—nothing.

T.   No fears?

P.   None. I felt a little insecure at times; then I tried to make the terror and anguish more pronounced. On the whole, it's not going . . . I don't feel very . . .

T.   What happened after you began to feel afraid and made an effort to increase your fears?

P.   They went away, actually. It's so comical.

T.   So are you telling me that after three sessions you've had no more panic attacks, no more fears, and that all that's left now is a bit of insecurity?

P.   Well, my fundamental insecurity is still there; every time that I have to do something I need to remind myself that I've got to try, because otherwise my wish to escape would prevail. But I really feel this need. I need to be completely my own master again, to be able to count on myself without needing . . . so . . .

T.   Did you ask for help?

P. No, I didn't, particularly in the past few days; on the contrary, I went to a few places on my own.

T. What places ? Where did you go, and where did you stay?

P. I went shopping for various things without having to find the usual excuses. On Saturday there was a children's festival; well, N. was there, too, so all of us—P. and I—went along, but then he left; I still had a cousin there with me, but I must say that the whole affair didn't particularly disturb me. I mean, I didn't find an excuse to leave my son there, as I would have done in the past, so . . . I should mention that it was an extremely crowded place, with lots of people. At first I didn't . . . I mean, I was rather . . . I didn't feel particularly ill physically, but a bit of visual sensitivity I think . . . But I never felt ill. I mean, at other times, I would at the least have had to find the keys to the car, and go and sit in the car . . . after I reached the car I used to feel better. But I didn't do that this time; I stayed on, perfectly calm. I'm feeling very well at present.

The session continued with redefinitions of the patient's different perception of the past and present, following the change in her management of fear.

T. Considering the results we have obtained, your problems were not so terrible, so invincible, or so absolutely immutable. It has only taken a little . . .

P. That's right.

T. . . . to change . . .

P. Of course.

T. . . . That is very important.

P. It's that I was probably dealing with it in the opposite way. When I think about it now, it seems to me that I always dealt with it by appealing to rationality, that is, by saying: "This problem is useless, you're not supposed to have it. . . ." In fact, at that time, I used to get very irritated when people said, "Make an effort, try to keep yourself in check," because I was very good at keeping myself in check, but I was never able to. . . .

Reframing Phobic Situations through Metaphor and Hierarchical Scale

T.   You can't put a cat in a bag.

P.   No.

T.   The more you push, the more you push, finally it will start scratching and get angry; the bag will break open, and it will come out furious. Instead, you have to let it out and educate it; learn to educate it and have a good relationship with it.

After this reframing of the change that had occurred, I constructed a base for the evolution of the therapy toward concrete experiences of overcoming fear-laden situations.

T.   Now, in that direction . . . I'd like to know all the things that you really would be afraid of doing now. Let's say on a hierarchical scale of 1 to 10, where number 10 is the thing that you would be most afraid of doing.

P.   The thing that absolutely scares me most, I believe, is the thought of taking the car and going far away, I mean, far, far, far away. Going away for a whole day. Being away from home, outside. But that, too . . . I mean it's strange, now, I don't know whether it depends on the fact that it happened last summer and I didn't . . . I mean, during my last vacation . . . I have never felt ill on a holiday, and yet I was far away from everyone, but I think I was so far removed from everything that I didn't have any schemes of reference. I mean, I didn't think that I was far away from home; I was away on vacation.

T.   . . . And there you don't think about anything.

P.   Instead, if I'm far from home because I'm in Arezzo, say, alone, I imagine that I'd be very disturbed at finding myself . . . it does in fact disturb me. And I imagine being far away from the car, far from the place where I'm going, far . . . anywhere.

The "Apple Prescription" Accompanied by Suggestive Tricks

T.   Good. So we must go through the trial of fire, right?

P.   Yes, you said that.

T.   You work on Saturday mornings, don't you?

P.   Yes.

T.   But can you take an hour off?

P.   Yes.

T.   Good. I'm only asking you to do one thing, on Saturday, from now until the next time we meet, but you must keep in mind everything that we have done, and every time you have a fear, you must try to exacerbate it; every time you want to avoid something, you must think that you can avoid avoiding, just like you can take the log with you, and all those things. . . .

Now, on Saturday morning you must take an hour off, leave the office, fetch your car, get into the car, but before stepping into the car you must do a pirouette . . . you must do it. . . . You come to Arezzo, and find a parking spot in the center. When you get out of the car, you must do another pirouette; then I want you to walk toward the center, and precisely toward the market, and go looking for the biggest, reddest, and ripest apple you can find. Only one apple. Then, since I will be here on Saturday morning working like a slave, you will come here, knock on the door, leave the apple for me, and go back home. Because I will go without lunch, and you will have to get me something to eat—only one apple: the biggest, reddest, ripest one you can find. Put it in a paper bag and leave it here for me. We will meet again at the next appointment. All right?

P.   I'll die on the way.

T.   I'll be expecting you on Saturday. O.K.?

P.   O.K.

FIFTH SESSION

T.   Well, well. I see that we have come alone this afternoon.

P.   No, I'm alone here, but . . .

T.   Oh . . . I see . . . If you had come alone . . . whew!

P.   You mean, "We're beginning to exaggerate a bit now."

T.   "We're beginning to be really good."

P.   No, but anyway—I don't know, I might have tried. I might have tried, but my parents had some things to do in Arezzo, so . . . I might have tried—maybe.

T.   Maybe? Well, we'll see about that.

P.   Because I brought you the apple, but it was no picnic.

T.   I can imagine that. I wouldn't have made you do it if it had been a picnic.

P.   The return trip was all right . . .

Redefining the Effects of the "Apple Prescription"

T.   Now, let's explain ourselves. Let's tell each other all about it. How did the story with the apple go?

P.   Apart from the fact that I hoped it would be raining really hard: "At least the market will be closed."

T.   So that there'd be fewer people?

P.   Then I hoped to catch the flu, which is something that can always happen in one's free time. Then I was undecided whether to take a whole day off and stay a couple of hours . . . or maybe leave at 8.30 A.M. and try to . . .

T.   To be sure that you'd get here.

P.   To make sure that I'd get here. But then I opted not to do any of those things because it would

have been tragic, from a certain viewpoint . . .
So I left. I forgot to do a pirouette as I stepped
into the car, so I got out again and did it—but
initially I forgot.

T.   Initially you forgot. That's very bad.

P.   [laughs] Very bad; I really forgot; I remembered
in Piazza Sant' Agostino and thought it wasn't a
good idea to drive back the whole way; then . . .

T.   How was your car trip after the pirouette?

P.   My trip after the pirouette was, well, quite un-
troubled, in the first part. I had taken care to
bring some music because that was the only
thing that could divert my thoughts now and
then. Part of the way—the part I had imagined
would make me feel worse, because my night-
marish question was, "What is going to happen
beyond the main road?" I mean something . . . I
mean, the moment one is just as far from the
arrival point as from the departure point, so that
one can't even turn back, because it would take
the same amount of time . . .

Use of Metaphor

T.   Like the donkey that was crossing a river and
stopped in the middle; there were crosscurrents,
and it didn't know what to do: "Shall I go ahead
or shall I go back?"

P.   At first I was rather . . . "Well, If I really can't make
it, I'll go back home." At that point, it wasn't possible anymore because it would have taken the
same amount of time. Then I became so anxious
. . . But why didn't I tell him that I don't like using
stairs, which would have been an easier task?
And then I tried to remind myself that getting here
wouldn't be the end of it because . . . considering what I was supposed to do later, it was so
depressing to think about going back . . . I felt
slightly comforted then. Anyway, except for the
situations I've mentioned, situations like that . . .

T.   Where did you park your car?

P.   At the post office parking lot—the closest on the

> way into town. But I had to wait, queue up, wait at the side, and finally I parked; I had to stop at a few traffic lights, so . . .

T. Then you walked all the way to the market.

P. All the way to the market. While desperately looking for a fruit stand, I thought you had tricked me: "There aren't any fruit stands! I'll have to walk through the whole market and there won't be any fruit stands."

T. Have they moved?

P. No, no. It's just that I don't know my way around the market.

T. I think the fruit stands are high up the hill.

P. Yes, yes. No, but at that point things were quite all right. Well . . .

T. But I have one criticism: the apple wasn't big enough. [laughing]

The session continued with a further redefinition of this important *corrective emotional experience* at a cognitive level. The goal was to enhance the patient's self confidence and awareness of her own resources. Then we proceeded to another prescription that had the aim of giving the patient more concrete experiences in overcoming fear-laden situations.

T. By now, avoiding to avoid has become a habit for you. You are very competent at doing it well. O.K.? Instead, You will have to do something really funny today—now. I will give you an appointment for next time; we will see each other next time as usual. But you will leave here before your husband comes back. Where is your husband waiting for you?

P. Somewhere around here.

Prescription Accompanied by Suggestive Tricks

T. Well, tell him to wait. You go out from here, go to the elevator, make a pirouette, go into the elevator, go down, make a pirouette, leave the building and, armed with pen and paper that I'll give you now (I want them back, O.K.?), good . . . and I want you to count all the paving stones on the street between my office and near the Pieve.

P.   By the Pieve? Is the Pieve the church . . .

T.   . . . with the high tower.

P.   That's right.

T.   I want to know how many paving stones. In a straight line.

P.   In a straight line?

T.   Exactly how many stones there are. The type of stone may change, but you must count them, one after the other, along a straight line.

P.   Along a straight line, not the whole area, in length let's say.

T.   Yes, in length, how many stones.

P.   Not to the door—to the corner of the church.

T.   That's right, and you write it down here, and bring me the piece of paper.

P.   Now?

T.   Now, immediately. You knock on the door and give it to me, with the pen and all.

P.   But I have a pen.

T.   Oh, but it's important that I give it to you.

P.   That way I'll feel more strongly obliged to bring it back.

T.   Moreover, in a place of your choice, since I always have voice problems, you must buy me a packet of mint tablets. Dietetic—otherwise I'll get fat.

P.   All right.

T.   Well, then . . . we'll say goodbye later, because you'll knock, and I won't even let you in because I'll be busy. You knock and leave me this, like you did with the apple. All right?

P.   O.K.

SIXTH SESSION

Redefining the
Prescription

T.   Now . . . the stones weren't right.

P.   I thought so. I must have lost the count about forty times.

T.   I've checked.

P.   But I did count them. The problem was that . . .
first of all, I didn't expect . . . I mean, I felt quite
confident when I left, because I thought I would
find the stones as soon as I walked out of this
building.

T.   Oh! But did you do a pirouette?

P.   Yes, yes, but I wasn't expecting the cobbled paving. I doubted that crying was the right thing to
do, so I opted to laugh—it's much more digni-
fied, anyway. Then I set off, trying not to attract
too much attention. I decided it was better to
count the stones ten by ten. I soon realized that
it would be better to count them ten by ten, and
then move a step ahead, instead of going 1, 2
. . . which was becoming difficult.

T.   That's a good method.

P.   After I realized what a sight I must be—counting the stones one by one, stopping, looking
down, then suddenly leaping over ten stones.
And so . . . doing it the other way was relatively
simple. Well, I still looked like somebody walking with her feet stuck to the ground, looking
down . . .

T.   At those large stones, huh?

P.   Yes, but there it was a step, a stone, a step, a
stone—you can take each step a little differently;
it was all right, anyway. The tragic thing was that
at one point, while my mind was set on counting the stones in a precariously balanced position, I was stopped by a girl who wanted to sell
me some perfume. [she laughs] "But I've got to
count the stones; I can't . . . I don't need it . . . I
don't need it." The whole thing was quite difficult . . . I took a sigh of relief when it was over.
I tried to remember how many stones there were
. . . I think I may have counted wrong by tens
or by hundreds . . . perhaps the units were . . .
by tens or by hundreds. I couldn't swear on it.

T.   On the contrary, I should tell you that your
mistake is in the order of units.

P.   Units?

T.   There's an error of three for the small stones and of six for the larger ones. [laughing]

P.   And, I repeat, it was difficult. In some places, the large stones . . . When one stone ends like this, and there's another—I don't know how to count that, because they form a perfect angle.

T.   Then maybe the count . . .

P.   And counting between people's legs is something difficult too; one man stood as if glued to the stones, and I couldn't count them because they couldn't go from here to there, so I had to take a different direction. And there were three or four stones in the asphalt at the crossroads.

T.   Those, too?

P.   I had a minor problem deciding whether to count them or not.

T.   How long did it take? Did it take you a long time?

P.   No, it didn't take me very long. Also because at one point I even got worried . . . I was running like a train. It must have been really comical to see this person walking around face down, oblivious of what was happening around her. People could have died of laughter on the street, for all I cared. I was intent on carrying out my mission, with absolutely ungraceful and rather insecure steps. Ungraceful it certainly was. It must have been a very moving sight, from an aesthetic point of view.

T.   You should have had some candy.

P.   On the contrary, I was very, very lucky with the candy. I was incredibly lucky with the candy, because I went into a . . . actually, coming out from here, I went into the first tobacconist's to buy some cigarettes, and they had the candies.

T.   But do you know why the shops in this area sell the low fat ones?

P.   Because you send your patients to buy them.

Redefining the Results   T.   So how was your week, after this . . .

P.   All right.

T. What do you mean by that?

P. Well, everything was pretty calm. I even carried out a bold deed today. I came . . . no, I didn't come here by myself, but I came in my own car, and brought my mother along. My mother, who is absolutely useless from that point of view . . .

T. Who, on the contrary, needs protection.

P. Yes. Plus my mother's friend, who is completely batty. So . . . I've been playing the social worker . . . taking them out for a ride . . . No, I mean, they had some things to do, and . . . I don't know what's worse, coming alone or in company . . . Anyway . . . I'm not saying that driving today was like driving five years ago, but it was already better than last time.

The session continued with a cognitive redefinition of the evidence of change and the patient's ability to deal with situations that she had previously avoided for many years. At this point, I also began to consider the change in the interrelational system that surrounded the patient, and proceeded to reframe the unavoidable loss of all the attention she had received from these people because of her pathology. The therapy thus evolved in the direction of changing the patient's attitudes in her relationships, as well as prescribing further concrete experiences without fear.

Prescription: Anthropologist in the Family

T. Well, well. Now, that makes me think of a very important thing that I will need. For next time, I want you to make detailed observations about the people around you, from a psychological, social, and anthropological point of view. We have never talked about them, and now is the time to do that. Therefore, I want to know about your whole family situation and how it has evolved. But I want you to tell me about it after having carefully observed, for one week, how these people behave and how they address you, without—if this is possible for someone as rational as you—without using too much rationality. The more superficial aspects; also because, as Oscar Wilde said, "The true mystery of the world is the visible, not the invisible." Therefore, observe. Only that.

P.   I just have one problem about next week. I work extended hours for the elections: What shall we do about that?

T.   Well, we'll find a solution.

P.   O.K.

Direct Prescription with Suggestive Tricks

T.   The other important thing is what you are going to do now. Since you have mentioned a certain "anticlericalism" on your part, I am, by now, well known for being "heretical," but I feel that since . . .

P.   Oh, but you can send me to religious functions! . . . I mean, it doesn't bother me at all to go to church.

T.   Since you have received a sort of miracle, we must sanctify the whole thing. To sanctify it, you are going to go out and do your usual pirouette in the elevator. You are going to go out and do something rather peculiar. You leave from here, turn right at the newspaper stand, walk straight on, turn at the end of the street and you will find a church, the Church of S., if I'm not mistaken; you enter the church, light a candle to I don't know which saint, take a holy picture, and walk back.

P.   What if there aren't any holy pictures?

T.   All churches have them. You walk back up to the church you have already seen and fulfill the same function: light a candle and take a holy picture. Then you walk downhill, and the last church is that of San Francesco, so you will also have the chance to admire some very beautiful churches. Light a candle, take a holy picture. Ring the bell when you get back here.

P.   No. [she laughs] I really don't mind churches. It's the religious functions . . .

T.   Ring the bell and leave everything here with me. [He makes the next appointment.]

P.   So. Four churches and four holy pictures, huh?

T.   Yes, but the ones that I've told you, all right? . . . [He asks for information.]

P.   What if they're closed? I need to get this right. [she laughs]

T.   You'll find the holy pictures. As I've already told you, rationality doesn't always work.

SEVENTH SESSION

Redefining the
Prescription

T.   So, the holy pictures, the postcards . . .

P.   They weren't exceptional. [she laughs]

T.   I have looked at them carefully. I liked the card of San Donato very much.

P.   All I could find at first was material on how to reserve 0.8 percent income tax to Catholic charities.

T.   "The Word is Life," Saint Donato. I appreciated this one. And this one: "Experience the Mission."

P.   The card inside was the same as . . . I only realized it after I had taken it. I got the small card at the Church of San Francesco. In the end I discovered that it had the same picture as the first booklet from the church down here.

T.   Good. Did we light the candles?

P.   Yes, and there was . . . Well, we lit one little lamp, one little candle like this, and two normal-size candles, because we even had the chance to pick and choose.

T.   Hmm, perfect. So how did it all go? How comical did we feel?

P.   Well, not very much, as I said, because, I mean . . . before I went in, it was all . . . by the way, they were saying the rosary at one of the churches; that was superlative. Because later. . .

T.   Did you join in?

P.   No, I didn't join in; my thing was, very spartan. There were no candles at the back; they were all up front, so I walked through the church accompanied by a "murmur of prayers"; I lit my candle and pretended to be very absorbed in the whole affair . . . The others—well, there were a lot of people admiring . . . there were a lot of tourists . . . One feels observed, even if one isn't participating for real. I don't see why they should have observed me with any more interest than they observed the other people coming in . . . Well, anyway . . . There was a monk—no, a priest—it crossed my mind that he was checking how long it took me, but then I told myself "I don't think so; I suppose they have strange visitors every day."

T.   Oh, well, yes, I believe so.

P.   Right. I left my offering, lit a candle, and took a holy picture; I was a prototype of the perfect Christian.

The session continued with a redefinition of the results obtained thus far, analyzing the patient's new lifestyle not only with respect to previously fear-laden situations but also to her relationships with other people.

P.   As I've told you, I was much better in the end than at the beginning, but that wasn't enough, because I wanted to feel better, but with those relapses . . . , they occurred much more rarely, but when they occurred I got even more upset.

T.   That's why it's necessary to think that a moment of inhibition, an occasional triggering of the process is useful; and we have to be able to get over it, because that's how we really learn not to fall into the trap again, because we have become more able to control it. Also because after our brain has formed the habit of doing certain things over many years, it will easily fall back into the same thing again.

I went on to define some further objectives to be reached: to transform what she had learned until then into spontaneous action; to change the interrelational system around her, which had thus far been defined by her need of help and other people's willingness to meet this need. I also redefined the evolving interrelational system and ended with the last prescription of the agoraphobia focal therapy.

Prescribing How to Anticipate Relapse

T.   Well, all right. At this point, the ritual question for me is, How could we ruin everything we have done so far?

P.   In what way? As an expression of will? What can I do to ruin everything? [silence] I don't know.

T.   Good. This week, then, there are no prescriptions, nothing to do except to continue avoiding to avoid. Do what you feel like doing. And you must repeat this thought: "How might I ruin everything I have done together with Dr. Nardone?"

P.   I'll find a solution.

T.   Even several.

P.   Really? They exist, do they?

T.   What could I do to ruin everything . . . I never stop baffling you, do I?

P.   And you think I want to start thinking about something like that?

T.   Yes. You must think about it.

EIGHTH SESSION

Redefining the Prescription

T.   So, have we thought about how we might ruin everything?

P.   Yes, I've thought about it; I haven't found many answers. First because one answer doesn't involve ruining anything, because things are bad enough already, when I don't feel well . . . but that isn't a way to ruin everything; it just happens. On the other hand, it's difficult for me to believe that I might deliberately make a mistake. That really isn't something I would decide. The only thing I thought could be a way of ruining

everything would be: "We have only been joking; things don't really work this way."

T. Would I be the one to say that?

P. Yes.

T. . . .

P. Yes, that's true.

T. But I could also say, "Yes, we've just been playing around; this isn't for real. You haven't recovered; all that you and I have done so far . . . You
are playing a trick on me."

P. No, that was in the beginning. But I didn't say
. . . Still, the fact remains that something has
happened. I came in with the car by myself
today. It wasn't a lot of fun.

T. And nobody had asked you to do it.

P. Nobody had asked me to do it, but I know that
I must avoid avoiding. I didn't really feel like
it . . . but it was enough to say, "I've got to." My
husband is usually at home in the afternoon, so
he comes along and takes the opportunity to do
other things in town. But today he couldn't, so I
would have had to say, "Yes." Instead I decided
not to ask him, even though I knew . . . Also, I
haven't been feeling well lately; probably my
health hasn't been very good. Although it isn't
. . . I feel worn out; we've been through the
whole election period . . . so I've lost some sleep,
and that kind of thing. It was a bit different from
the other trip, when I had ups and downs that
would look like this on a graph: the lowest point
at the outstart, when I felt absolutely terrified;
then a constantly rising line, as I traveled for
more than ten kilometers and saw that everything was going well; then a steep drop again. I
felt really miserable at one point, but then this
time I felt a nip in the stomach during the whole
trip—it wasn't particularly painful, but latent.
But I got here. Not in absolutely perfect condition, but still.

> T. Where did you park?
> P. At a parking lot near here.
> T. You found it?
> P. Yes, I found it. I'm incredibly lucky these days! I even find parking spaces when they're all full.
> T. Everything is going well.

After this evaluation, I proceeded to reanalyze all the changes that had occurred in the patient's relationship with others, and to redefine this relationship. I also started to explain the type of work we had done to date, to make the patient aware of the techniques I had used during the therapy with the goal of completing therapy. This session closed without any prescriptions.

NINTH SESSION

The patient reported no problems related to fear. She reported that some interactional problems had emerged within the family, so the whole session was spent on reframing the new balance to be built up with her relatives, without the fear. Together, we evaluated the results of our work.

> T. What has concretely changed in your life in the past nine weeks?
> P. What has concretely changed? That I am again able to do a lot of things that I had stopped doing before. That's the essential thing.
> T. So what has changed in concrete terms?
> P. Things are going better.
> T. Has there been a change in your quality of life?
> P. Yes. In this period my quality of life has certainly changed, undoubtedly. The quantity, too, in the sense of . . . how much more life I am experiencing when I don't stay closed in, with my wish to get around.
> T. I would say so. Now, percentagewise—if we were to calculate the percentage, of what part of your problems we have resolved, what do you think?

P. Ninety-five.

T. What?

P. Ninety-five.

T. More than what I said?

P. I think the remaining 5 percent is related to a stable result. I mean: I feel that what's missing now is the "stabilizer," which means. . . .

T. To make it permanent.

P. To make it permanent.

T. To do that, there's the little staircase that we were talking about, and above all, we need to establish a new balance in your relationships with the people around you, which is still to be studied. Therefore, I now want you to study accurately what could be the best relationship with these persons, what it has been like so far, how we can construct it, and continue to avoid avoiding, and above all avoid letting the bad habit return. Not the fear—the bad habit.

TENTH SESSION

P. All right.

T. What do you mean by "all right"?

P. In the sense that I didn't have any great problems with doing anything.

T. Like what?

P. Getting around . . . it was as if I had a different attitude; I forgot that I needed to make an effort to do things. I just did them.

Redefining the Changes in View of an Ending of the Therapy

T. Can we say that the problems are more than 95 percent resolved today?

P. Yes, certainly.

T. Where are we, at 99.9 percent?

P. Yes, yes, yes. Yes. There will always be some moments. . . .

After this last evaluation, the therapy ended with a final redefinition and reincentivation.

Incentives
toward
Personal
Autonomy

T.   I'll always be here. That . . . I always make the following agreement with people: when a therapy is over, it does not mean that I have closed my door and don't want to see that person again. On the contrary, it means that all you have to do is call, if there's any problem, and I guarantee that I will see you as soon as possible, that same day or at the most within two days. That is a guarantee . . .

P.   All right.

T.   I believe that you will have absolutely no need for that, but it's important that you know.

P.   Yes, it's much more reassuring.

T.   Just like it is important to plan a series of appointments at much longer intervals, which really serve as a checkup on the situation.

P.   Yes.

T.   One thing that it is very important to emphasize now is the fact that even if I have used some rather strange methods . . . with some techniques that are a little persuasive, and so on, as I have told you at other times, I have done nothing more than stimulate your personal resources. It's not that I've added something that wasn't there before to your vessel. I have just brought out something that was already there, which had become stuck. So the answer . . . after all, the whole change is thanks to you.

P.   Let's look at it that way.

T.   I was only . . . like a diamond cutter who brings out a very beautiful stone from the rough stone. He has to strike a little at the right places, not too strongly nor too gently, because the diamond might break, or there would be no effect, until he brings out the gem with all its facets. That's all I have done, but the stone was already there, because I couldn't have invented a diamond . . .

P.   You're the one who's saying it! I won't doubt it, God forbid.

T. Now it is important that the diamond continue to shine, and not to want to throw it back into the mud.

P. Uh, huh.

T. I don't think any great effort is needed for this. It's enough to let it shine. Well, we will meet again in three months for the follow-up, and remember: a diamond doesn't need to make an effort to shine.

7

Ritual and Counter-Ritual:
A Case of Phobic-Obsessive Compulsions

FIRST MEETING: THE PATIENT'S PARENTS COME IN

Defining the Problem

Father. M., who is now 17 years old, is repeating his second year at the *Liceo Scientifico*. Now . . . I'm going to try to recapitulate a long process, which began two years ago when . . . that's why I didn't want to bring the boy in here with us. M. knows only part of the story.

T. Of course.

F. M. was found in a car by the police, in the company of a person . . . in a car, with a person of the same sex . . . as grown up as I, or maybe even a little older . . . who, it turned out, was our dearest family friend, and who had been enticing him for some time. Such encounters, as we might call them, had occurred more than once. Those encounters were clearly of a homosexual kind; things were apparently limited—if we can call it that—to situations of masturbation, or even oral ones, mutually, in that sense. Now, since that person was tried in court . . . and convicted (the case went before a Court of Appeals), but this episode has been sufficiently . . . let's say . . . About seven or eight months after that happened M. started having crises . . . because I was at my studio and my wife used to call and say, "Come; M. is getting out of hand here"; he was starting then; he started closing himself inside a wardrobe, didn't want to meet anybody ever again . . .

F. In therapy we talked about how this came to happen, and he said, "Because of this and that, partly because I was afraid you'd find out that the guy had been feeling me up." In the end, he had . . . let's say this person had [he snorts] access to M., who consented to the situation. Anyway, after that story ended with the intervention of the police, and seven or eight months had passed . . .

Investigating the T. Did this become public knowledge?
Parents' Perceptive- F. No, no.
Reactive System and the M. No.
Attempted Solutions, If T. Was it a very secret thing?
Any, Particularly in F. Yes, between ourselves.
Relation to the Social T. Did the intervention of the police not cause . . .
Context F. [interrupting the therapist] It did not cause anything because . . .

T. [continues his question, interrupting the father] . . . in the social context . . .

M. It was a closed-doors affair, doctor.

F. In the social context ? No, because among other things the police of our district are my friends; I know them. The captain took care of this question, so there were no problems from that point of view. Now, as I was saying, six to eight months after this had happened, M. started showing abnormal signs. This also occurred coincidentally with the fact that his umpteenth motorbike had been stolen a couple of days before, and that his grandmother, my mother, had recently died. After a few days, we started worrying and took him to a doctor. He stayed in bed for about ten days—six, seven, eight days, ten days—and then, finally convinced, we went to a professor in N., a neuropsychiatrist . . .

M. [interrupting] On February 5th it was a year . . .

F. . . . who at first diagnosed an obsessive psychosis, but later said, "No, maybe this is a borderline case." Anyway, he prescribed Semac [Orap] tablets, a product sold in the Vatican City, a product . . . oh, but very, very bland, almost a therapeutic dose, half a tablet once a week when it's usually two to three tablets a week . . .

M. [interrupting] Only a quarter, at times.

F. At times only a quarter of a tablet. And three drops of Psicoperidol, and some Anafranil, one tablet—pediatric doses, one might say. But then in February he advised us . . . he says, "Let's do this: by August, M. and school . . . maybe it would be a good idea if you tried to give your family a move." Taking advantage of the fact that in the summer I usually go to I. to practice my profession as a painter until the end of October, he said, "Let's do this: why don't you move to I. earlier." So I signed him up to do the second semester in school there in I. He went to school for one month, but after that he couldn't deal with it anymore, he didn't want to be with other people. Just think, M. has friends—a lot of friends, many people who are fond of him, especially there, in that area, people who think well of him—in short, who are fond of him, and who have stayed close to him. He used to go to discos, but then . . .

M. [interrupting] He hated crowds.

F. He used to come back [with strong emphasis] and say, "I can't bear to *stay* there." When spring

arrived, and at a certain point I . . . yes, he was
really ill . . . I gradually took away those medicines—but the medicines weren't all administered to him at the same time. First one, then
the other, then the other. And so, with the advent
of spring and his friends, one might say . . .

M. Provided some distraction . . .

F. Some distraction. He said he'd had quite a good
summer. Although I should mention that meanwhile, at home, his problem was, one might say,
one word: there's AIDS, AIDS . . .

M. [interrupting] Blood. He can't bear to see even a
tiny drop of blood . . .

F. Blood, AIDS, a needle on the ground—and he
used to take baths—two, three baths a day with
shampoo, foams he used, bottles and bottles of
shampoo . . .

M. He washes and doesn't dry himself.

F. Shampoos [emphatically] . . .

M. The towels are no good . . .

F. [interrupting] Wait a moment, that was at the
beginning . . .

M. [continues, interrupting in turn] . . . the glasses
are no good, the plates, the forks—I feel like I'm
going crazy, running around the house trying to
please him, and now he is—excuse me [to her
husband who has tried to interrupt her]—he is
reverting to this time last year, when we went
away to make him calm down.

F. [interrupting; to the therapist] May I smoke a
cigarette?

T. Yes.

M. He took to his bed and wouldn't move. Part of
my efforts, Doctor, are on food; he likes all those
fancy foods, which goes to show that he is a bit
strange in everything he does. And, as I was saying, now he's reverting to the same period last
year. He takes . . . bottles of rubbing alcohol—
they can get sick, they're no good anymore,

we've got to buy a new one because that one has gotten sick. And the same with cigarettes, because he smokes a lot. Now, next month he will be 17.

T.   So he attributes a sort of . . . liveliness, of vitality to things? He animates objects? The bottle got sick, so to speak?

Investigating the Patient's Perceptive-Reactive System as Seen by the Parents

F.   Oh, yes. The bottle is sick, and the packet must have fallen down onto the floor, so it got sick, and so did the lighter. I want to try to recall for a minute. Now . . . in the summertime he was reasonably well. He abandoned that problem with shampoos, bidets, and so on, and that, let's say, excessive hygiene, and spent that whole period reasonably well. He was still concerned with those little things, the glass, say, the fork— but it was tolerable. Then we went back to N.; more precisely, my wife went to N. first, so . . .

M.   [interrupting] To make him go to school, so he could repeat the year.

F.   To start school, while I was supposed to stay there in October and work. But I was called away because M. started feeling bad again. Meanwhile, he had been attending school. I went back to N. earlier than planned and then . . . on the way to school . . . [he corrects himself] on the way to a disco M. had an accident. He should have the splint removed soon; perhaps they'll remove it next week. He had an accident and stayed in the hospital for an operation; I was "hospitalized" with him because for sixteen days I could not leave him, night or day, because he didn't want me to leave—with enormous difficulties taking food back and forth . . .

M.   [interrupting] He doesn't want, to go to the bathroom if it isn't his own bathroom at home.

F.   "What is this standing on? What's that placed against?" All those kinds of things. Then, after the hospital, during convalescence, which he . . .

M.   [interrupting] At home . . .

F.   The problem is that now he has started with that bidet again. . . . Now he has quit . . .

M.   He won't dry himself, he doesn't . . .

F.   Now he has quit. . . . yes, because maybe the towel has been put in the wrong place . . .

M.   Oh, let me tell you one more thing before I forget; suddenly, the bed, completely clean, with all the bedclothes just changed . . .

F.   [interrupting] He sees a tiny drop . . .

M.   No, no, even if it isn't there. He's jumpy as a cat: you've got to throw away those towels, change the pillow and pillowcase and I don't know what else; the sheets, all those kinds of things.

T.   Right. So his main symptoms now are ideas, obsessions about dirt, about contamination . . .

F.   Now he makes himself vomit, which is what he was doing a year ago . . .

M.   [interrupting] With his toothbrush, all the time, Doctor, he does it all the time . . .

F.   Seven, eight times, even. He makes himself throw up, and if he doesn't succeed, he'll eat something to provoke the vomiting . . .

M.   [interrupting] Yes, he goes into the kitchen. But, Doctor, I've noticed that in the past few days— actually the past fifteen days or more—he's become much more insistent, just like last year. But he reacts this way: he calls up his father at the studio, because he wants to stay at home, and goes over to the studio; but he's a very unruly boy. He was like that already as a child, Doctor, I feel it's important to point this out. My husband thinks maybe that has nothing to do with it. Unfortunately, there are precedents on both sides of the family; on my side and my mother's: a sister who was traumatized by her husband who mistreated her for things that were all still to happen, and unfortunately I have a sister who is violent toward my mother. My son has done

it—does it with me sometimes; at times he becomes fixated and says he's got to kill me. He
isn't doing that anymore, maybe thanks to this
injection that we're giving him . . .

F.   Mobiten, half a vial a month—only this month,
since he was insisting with that kind of behavior, he's been given half a vial twice . . .

M.   At very close distance, really, between injections.

T.   The psychiatrist again?

F. and M.   Yes, him again.

F.   I have some prescriptions here that you may
want to take a look at. [He takes the prescriptions out of his pocket and gives them to the
therapist.]

M.   He says this is a serious thing, Doctor. He says
it's a big thing, as if the boy had gone backward
by three or four years.

F.   He . . . M. says no, I am sure that . . . now, I
would like to consider for a moment . . .

M.   He was really looking forward to coming here,
to you.

F.   Yes, just a moment, that . . . when he saw you
on the Maurizio Costanzo Show, he immediately
called me. He says, "Dad, I'm listening to something very interesting. Maybe Dr. Nardone is the
person who can solve my problems."

M.   He'll help me do it, he'll help me.

F.   So we went out and bought your book and read
it; I just read some passages, so . . .

M.   [interrupting] Yes, because he isn't able to read.

F.   He became very enthusiastic about it; it's very
important to him, and this fact is surely . . .

T.   Positive.

F.   He says: "When I get well, I'll throw a big party."
[The therapist gives the prescription forms back
to the father.]

F.   From a practical standpoint, after all, he has
support from me, his mother, his friends; soon,

when the good season comes, we'll probably go back to I., and maybe he . . .

M. But that will, at the most, provide a distraction, Doctor.

F. He says he's always thinking about these things, always the same things . . .

M. Contagion. Lately he hasn't insisted on the bidet, but on putting alcohol on his lips; if you look has lips you'll see they're chapped.

F. He's quit with the bidet.

M. And he vomits. And the alcohol must go onto the bidet. I have to clean it before he washes himself, and then he no longer dries himself with a towel anymore. He walks around with all the soap dripping down from between his legs.

F. Another thing that needs to be said . . . this pressing, particularly pressing condition—I don't know . . . among other things, he's been walking with a leg that is . . . for four months now. He's been in hospital . . . he can't walk around . . .

M. Yes, but he doesn't behave any better when he's on the street; he was behaving worse.

F. Yes, I understand, I meant . . . And this pressing situation began coincidentally—no, as soon as he heard that we could come here to you, a few days after we had seen you on the Maurizio Costanzo Show, and you told me . . . this and that . . . So we decided . . . By the way, it seemed to me that this is a . . . last summer M. had . . . ten, twelve sessions with a psychiatrist and psychotherapist, but then in July and August he was on vacation and we were supposed to meet again in September. But then in September M. decided to stay in I., because he hadn't established much of a relationship—he was getting individual therapy. M. says, "But we spend hours there, and sometimes we don't even say a word" . . . so it doesn't seem that he had . . . although

I should mention that he almost instantly quit taking those baths in the bathtub thanks to a bet he made with a doctor. He said, "I'm going to win this bet," and from that moment he did, in fact, almost completely stop doing that.

M. Doctor, there's one thing that I've been meaning to say. Ever since he was born, this boy . . . because let's admit that . . . my husband says no, but . . . [to the husband] you and I didn't get along very well in the past, and maybe that's why the boy turned out that way, why he gave himself to that man; I don't know. What I do know is that this boy has caused me a lot of worries ever since he was born.

M. Here is a letter that M. left us—here. [he holds out the letter to the therapist] That was around . . . last November, er . . . around last November, right? Last November, after . . . no, was it in November the year before?

M. Yes, in 1988.

F. Yes, in 1988, when we still hadn't quite understood this question, but had noticed that he wasn't going to school; I don't know . . . drinking wine, smoking. Oh, I got very angry, and told him when he came home, and so . . . here, he left us. . . . [he points to the letter]
[Pause. The therapist reads the letter.]

Focusing on the Problems in the Couple's Relationship

T. Here. What does he mean by the fact that you've never made a . . . serious decision?

F. I wouldn't know how to explain that. I wouldn't know how to explain it because . . . clearly, we've known each other for thirty years, but . . . there are some great divergences in our ideas, our characters . . . particularly . . .

T. Do you fight very often?

F. Yes, we have, we have.

T. Violently, too?

F. Yes, yes, yes, yes.

T. Hmm, I see. Still?

F.   Well, now, in the present, let's say—no, not anymore. It's been a while now.

M.   We're really exhausted. We've got more important problems. I mean, he's very harsh with me, that's true. . . .

F.   [interrupting] Well, but it's simply a matter of divergences, just . . . I mean, these things remain . . .

M.   He's very harsh . . .

Construction of the Therapeutic Relationship

T.   You seem to be too absorbed by his problems.

M.   Of course! At least I am, for my part.

P.   We are too absorbed by his problems.

T.   To have space.

M.   Yes, yes.

F.   But we sometimes still . . . but that is due to the fact that we certainly have different outlooks on life, on existence.

M.   [interrupting] Doctor, may we tell the doctor an anecdote?

T.   Of course.

M.   Two years ago, when my husband went to work in I. for the first time, and this . . . this fact, let's say . . . I blamed him for it, right? I remember that B. had only just turned 14; we were in I. and he wanted the keys to our house. M. had already left home; he wanted the keys . . .

F.   [interrupting] M. was living in P.

M.   He was in P., so the house was empty and locked, and I didn't want a boy of 14 to have the keys to our house and be able to go there alone. Later on, he confessed that he had taken someone home with him . . . while my husband was . . .

F.   [interrupting] He can't have been making any big movements, because I used to go there often . . .

M.   You give him the keys, just give him the keys. . . .

Investigating the Son's Relational Life

T.   Have you ever found out whether he's had any relationships with girls? Or only with men?

M. Yes, the boy has confessed to this.

F. Only with . . . ?

T. With men, or also with women? Has he ever been together with women?

F. M.?

M. Yes, he's had his little girlfriends.

F. He always had a little girlfriend before . . . and afterward, too. He's had girlfriends . . . then he says . . . "my heart isn't on it" because . . . this and that . . .

M. [interrupting, suggesting the beginning of a sentence] Yes, because with this fact . . .

F. He's quite successful, actually . . .

T. [interposing] Who does he fight with most?

F. Pardon me?

T. Which of you two does he argue the most with? With you or with her?

F. With her.

M. With me he's had some strong crises, during which he's even reached the point of hitting me, even grabbing a knife, as he did in I. last year in March, with the injections in his arm; he went: "I've got to kill you and not Dad, because Dad is stronger; you are weaker and I can do it with you, because I will acquire a strength I can't control." I used to take this position (she crosses her arms over her chest and squats), and let him hit me just so that he would calm down, and then at last I would take our little dog and run out of the house, because he used to grab the dog by its throat . . .

F. [interposing] But he isn't always like that; it's possible to play with B.; he is intelligent, too . . .

M. [interposing] He is loving and very sensitive, but he's scary when he has a crisis.

T. Very well. I understand. Now I'd like to see the boy.

F. and *M.*   Certainly.

T. All right?

F.   [rising] I . . . thought it was necessary to give you this exposition.

T.   [has risen and is walking toward the couple] I should say that it's been extremely important. [accompanies the parents to the door; the two are talking among themselves]

[The parents exit. The patient comes in.]

Together, the Therapist and the Patient Redefine the Problem and Construct a Therapeutic Relationship that is Different from the Relationship Prescribed by the Family System

T.   Now, your parents have explained the situation in general, to some extent. Obviously, it is important for me to learn about the situation, in very clear terms, from you. You are in therapy, for certain things . . .

P.   [interrupting] Nothing, the situation . . . I mean, I don't know . . . it disturbs me; let's say it disturbs me very much and is related to . . . they're all fixations related to the problem of AIDS; these . . . these things that create these problems for me . . . I don't know . . . which I've already explained—like, for example, I do all those . . . I get upset if the dog licks me on the mouth, so I go to the bathroom and use the toothbrush to make myself throw up. I mean, I do all these things . . .

T.   You're afraid of AIDS.

P.   Oh, yes.

T.   The toothbrush . . . [pause], the vomit . . . [pause].

P.   Yes. The various washings, using the bidet, washing my hands, stuff like that.

Investigating the Patient's Perceptive-Reactive System

T.   Therefore I suppose you must . . . carefully wash everything that has been used in certain exchanges.

P.   I don't understand.

T.   I suppose [pause] . . . you have to carefully wash [pause] . . . everything that has been used in certain types of sexual exchanges.

P.   Oh, yes.

T.   Because that's where the risk lies, right?

P.   Yes.

T.   I put it well, huh? I've got that right. As you can see, I'm much more direct . . .

P.   Yes, yes.

T.   So, mainly, you're careful to clean all that has been used during that type of sexual intercourse.

P.   Aha!

T.   Right?

P.   Yes.

T.   Because there's the risk of AIDS, because . . .

P.   [interrupting] I was traumatized by what happened.

T.   Oh, I can imagine! Uh, huh. Now tell me, how do you clean all the areas that have been used in one kind of sexual intercourse?

P.   With soap and water, or rubbing alcohol; for example, I even get to the point of drinking the alcohol, drinking a little bit of rubbing alcohol, and then I put the toothbrush here in my mouth, to throw up. And afterward I sometimes even put alcohol on my . . . on my penis and wash myself with soap; I mean, I rarely do it only with alcohol; but what's most pressing is the vomiting. I vomit every day.

T.   Of course.

P.   Many times, even. Even six, seven, eight times a day.

T.   Listen. After the story that your parents have told me about, have you had any other stories of that kind?

P.   No, no.

T.   But that story seems to have left its mark on you.

P.   Yes.

T.   So you interpreted that you had caught AIDS in those moments?

P.   Yes, but that terror has vanished by now because . . . I've had various tests, stuff like that. So I'm healthy.

T.   But the obsessive ritual has remained.

P.   Yes.

T. So all the rituals are to disinfect you of this fear? Hmm, hmm, How have you tried to fight these things?

P. It's partly a question of willpower, but I haven't been able to do it; it's so much stronger than me, it's too. . . . it's much stronger than me. I can't do it.

T. Things are more or always like this.

P. Yes, they are, in fact.

"Mind-Reading" Technique

T. Uh, huh. Listen, and this question of willpower . . . you say: I mustn't do it I mustn't do it I mustn't do it, I mustn't do it; the more you say it, the more you do it, right?

P. That's right.

T. Uh, huh.

P. Just like you wrote in your book too.

T. The harder you try not to do it, the more you do it, right?

P. Yes.

T. And what have the other attempted solutions been?

P. About the washing—that kind of thing?

T. Yes, yes.

P. Oh, I don't know . . . I don't know, disinfection of the hands, that kind of stuff . . . sometimes in the face; they're always, always the same kinds of washings . . . I don't know . . . the feet, disinfecting the feet, that kind of thing, for example sometimes . . . I don't know . . . they're always the same things, always the same.

T. Hmm. I see. Good. And . . . apart from that, are you beset by any other serious or nonserious problems?

P. No.

T. What's your relationship with your parents like?

P. We can say it's a good relationship for—a good relationship. Only that, for example, I'm scared of even just exchanging a cigarette with them,

and I'm afraid with them the same way. I don't
let them . . . put their mouths close to mine,
things like that; we never even kiss anymore,
things like that, because I'm afraid of them the
same way—that they might infect me.

T.   How are things with other people?

P.   Yes, with everybody.

T.   So you don't touch anybody anymore?

P.   Anymore . . . no, I do touch, but then I go and
wash myself—things like that . . . I mean, I've
always got to wash myself afterward.

T.   And do you see people, or do you stay isolated?

P.   No, I see people.

T.   Hmm, who do you see? Friends, other teenag-
ers . . .

P.   Friends—other boys and girls.

T.   Do you have a girlfriend?

P.   No, not right now.

T.   When you had a girlfriend—if you had one—
then you were more afraid, weren't you?

P.   I've had girlfriends, I've even had a lot of them.
It's just that I was always tied down by the fact
that, er, let's say . . . I don't know . . . I had to
. . . I would kiss the girl and then later I would
have to go and throw up—that kind of thing.
Before I didn't. I mean before, long before, a
couple of years ago, when I was seeing a girl I
didn't worry about these things, but now I do;
when I kiss a girl, I've got to go and throw up—
that kind of thing.

T.   Hmm.

P.   That's what it was like, at least until the end of
last month . . . this summer, because now I've
got a broken leg, so . . .

T.   Uh, huh. So we know that your basic symptom
serves the purpose of protecting you from the
terror of catching AIDS.

P.   Yes.

T.   Even though you don't have AIDS, because . . .

P.   No, no.

T.   But, you say, you might still catch it . . .

P.   Yes, yes.

T.   Because it's everywhere.

P.   Uh, huh.

T.   So your fear of catching it is so strong that you've got to sterilize yourself continuously.

P.   Yes!

T.   You've certainly discovered a great strategy for avoiding AIDS!

P.   Uh, huh! [he laughs]

Reframing the
Symptomatic Behavior
as Useful, and Making
Use of Humor

T.   I say, that way we can be sure you won't catch it!

P.   Yes.

T.   It's optimal. We should start divulging it, spreading first the fear, and then this strategy of yours among people, right?

P.   Uh, huh.

T.   First rinse your mouths with rubbing alcohol, then vomit, making yourself vomit every time you do something; wash yourselves, sterilize your penises in a terrible way—for men; as for women, we'll have them putting sodium hydroxide in their vaginas . . .

P.   [laughs]

T.   And so on, huh? A good solution!

P.   You're pulling my leg, huh?

T.   No. It's a good solution! [pause]. . . . If we take away this solution—what happens then?

P.   I don't think anything will happen. Things stay the same, they stay . . . they remain identical, I mean . . . nothing happens.

T.   Hmm. You wouldn't be more damaged if you were able to remove the symptoms?

P.   I don't really understand your question.

T.   Isn't it that you might be more damaged, that is, you might get worse—your fear, AIDS, or other things, if you stopped performing the rituals?

P. No, I don't think so; I don't think so.

T. Hmm. How many times a day do you do this to yourself?

P. The vomiting began as a joke; it had been many months since I made . . . since I made myself vomit. The whole story began as a joke; I pretended that I was going to kiss the dog or something like that, but the dog really did kiss me; that is [he emphasizes], it seemed to me that it really had kissed me and . . . I went and threw up. We can say that's how it started, and it went on and on.

T. You have a dog?

P. Yes.

T. What kind of dog is it?

P. Yorkshire.

T. Nice . . . what's the best way to sterilize oneself? Is it rubbing alcohol, or is there anything better?

P. No, alcohol, I always use alcohol. But then, the alcohol can get sick too, you know. It can get sick too.

T. It can get sick, too? It can get sick, too?

Use of Humor Again, and of Paradox

P. Oh, yes.

T. Then you really have a problem, if it gets sick, too. So, isn't there anything better that doesn't get sick?

P. Oh, no.

T. You haven't found anything better!

P. No.

T. There might be something better, mightn't there?

P. I don't know.

T. No? You don't think so?

P. Yes, I think so—something that disinfects more? I don't know, some medical disinfectant, I don't know. Maybe they have them at the hospital.

T. Hmm . . . Or something even better?

P. . . .

T. No, fire—you could use fire, couldn't you?

P. Oh, but fire is a problem.

T. Well, well, well. So how do you proceed, every-time you do these things to yourself? What do you do to make yourself vomit?

P. Oh, first I apply rubbing alcohol to my mouth; I take the bottle and apply alcohol to my mouth; then I put the toothbrush in, if I've had some-thing to eat; otherwise I even go and eat some-thing, I even eat something so that I can vomit. Then I take the toothbrush and put it in my mouth, and make myself vomit.

P. Uh, huh.

T. And sometimes I even . . . I even put it in my mouth first and then drink a little, and then vomit right away.

T. The alcohol?

P. Yes.

T. Is it good, the way it tastes?

P. [laughs] No, it's absolutely disgusting, alcohol.

T. It's absolutely disgusting. And what do you do to sterilize your penis?

P. I pour a little alcohol on it and then I put soap on and . . . it burns.

T. And it burns [pause] . . . so you need to feel a burn.

P. Yes, yes.

T. If you don't feel it burning, you don't think it's sterilized.

P. Oh, yes, yes, yes.

T. So it is necessary to feel some pain.

P. Yes. It's a self-damaging kind of behavior.

T. If you don't feel a little pain, then it isn't steril-ized. Uh, huh. I understand. [pause] Yes, it's quite a problem. It's a very complicated problem.

P. All these . . . Do you think it can be resolved?

T. I think I have some very good strategies. I don't know whether you'll be able to follow them.

Use of Paradox

P. [interposes] Because I admire you very much . . . I have a lot of faith in you.

T. How can you have that if you haven't . . .

P. [interposing with passion] I don't know, I have a lot of faith. The first time I saw you, I said, "Maybe this person can make me well"—something like that. Take away, really take away these fixations from me so that I can continue a normal life, as it was before . . . actually, it wasn't all that normal before either. But a normal life just like everybody else, like you and other people.

T. And you've been reading my book a little?

P. Yes, in parts. I've read parts of it.

T. What parts have you read?

P. Oh . . . the part in which . . . about the obsessive disorders. It's about obsessive disorders.

T. When you read about what I make people do, what effect did that have on you?

P. Oh, I don't know . . . sort of a strange effect. . . . I mean, I don't see any . . . I don't see how . . . you hit the mark, almost . . . how can I say this . . . how they can . . . I mean how they can work, but I think . . . these things . . .

T. How many times do you play your little game— how many times a day, more or less?

P. What little game?

T. Of vomiting, washing your penis, your hands and the rest.

P. No, maybe . . . in this period I am vomiting, I'm leaving the penis out a bit, not washing in the bidet so much. I only disinfect my penis once in a while. I did it more before, more before. Now I don't. Instead, what I do incessantly is vomit.

T. Listen; in your opinion, apart from protecting you from AIDS, what type of balance does your illness keep; in what way is it useful?

Reframing the
Symptom: Its
Relational Usefulness

P. I have no idea. None, in my opinion.

T. On the contrary, I see great usefulness in it. And not just for you, but for your whole family.

P.   Maybe a balance . . . the balance of the family, maybe.

T.   Uh, huh.

P.   The balance of the family, in the sense that if it wasn't for my problem, it might be a family that . . . I don't know. I have no idea. Maybe it seems to me that they don't get along too well.

T.   Uh, huh. I have read a letter that your parents brought me, which you wrote to them; mainly, I've heard that they argue, they argue a lot?

Focusing on the Parents' Arguments and on the Function of the Symptom

P.   Yes, In fact now his problem has arisen . . .

T.   Therefore your problem is useful!

P.   Yes, maybe it's useful, but I want to come out of it, Doctor, I can't bear this anymore. That's why I have come here. Because I want to come out as soon as possible.

Agreeing on the Modalities of the Treatment

T.   Hmm, hmm, Well, well. So you have read, you have seen that my methods are a bit unusual, right? I make people do strange, rather funny things, but they must be carried out absolutely without questions. I will give you the explanations. At a suitable time. All right?

P.   Yes, yes.

Prescription: Thinking that the Symptom is Useful to the Family's State of Equilibrium

T.   Now. First, this week I want you to think much as possible about the fact that your symptom is useful, essential for your family, and that changing it means throwing everything off balance. Therefore, I want you to think that your symptom is useful. And that it is very dangerous to change it.

P.   I understand.

T.   All right?

P.   Yes.

T.   So I want you to think intensely about this thing, all right?

P.   Yes.

Prescription of the Paradoxical Ritual

T.   Moreover, I want you to do the little game that you have read about, with the alarm clock, the half hour. But I will explain it better now. I mean that from now until we meet again, every day, you will take an alarm clock. Have you an alarm clock?

P.   Yes.

T.   You lock yourself alone in a room, find a totally comfortable position, draw the curtains in semi-darkness, set the alarm to go off after half an hour, and in that half hour you think about all the anguish, all the worst fears that come to your mind: of having AIDS, of having caught it, of having done this and that to yourself, all the worst things you can imagine, and do anything that comes into your mind: if you feel like rolling on the floor, then roll; if you feel like breaking something, break it. When the alarm rings, you turn it off; it's all over. You go back to your usual day. Every day, more or less at the same time. What time can you do it?

P.   Er . . . when . . .

T.   Let's say between half past two and three o'clock. Every day. OK?

P.   I understand.

T.   It's important that no one disturb you; don't explain what it is that you have to do. You say "the doctor prescribed it," and do it. All right?

P.   I mustn't say anything to my parents about what you've told me?

T.   No. This is a secret between me and you. O.K.?

P.   Yes.

T.   And this is the important thing every day. During the day, instead, I want you to think that your symptoms are extremely useful; they have a function, they keep a balance that it is dangerous to change.

P.   Yes.

T.   All right?

P.   Yes, yes.

T.   We will meet again in a week, and you will tell me everything you've been up to. All right?

P.   Yes.

[The patient exits. The parents reenter.]

T.   Now I have seen the situation; I have considered it. It is clearly a symptomatology of the obsessive-compulsive type, more or less like the ones you have seen described in my book. I would say that it is a very complicated, very severe problem, but this does not mean that the solutions have to be equally complicated, heavy, and painful. The important thing is to find the right key; sometimes, when the key is right, everything opens up in a very quick and resolutive manner. It's a question of finding the right key. I have started working with him; I have already given him prescriptions; I have carried out some maneuvers; what I do with him remains between me and him; from you I need a great deal of collaboration.

Capturing the Parents
by Elevating Them to
the Rank of Cotherapists

F. and M.   [nod in assent] Yes.

T.   In the sense that I also need you to carry out what I ask you to do.

M.   Of course.

T.   The first thing that I ask of you is this: just as you have, so far, done such a good job at controlling him, staying close to him, now you should become even better at taking a distance: if he vomits, he vomits; if he performs rituals, he performs rituals. You must absolutely get into an atmosphere of a conspiracy of silence. . . .

M.   At times, in fact, we do scold him. . . .

T.   A conspiracy of silence regarding the problems. . . .

F.   And when he requests our intervention, for anything?

M.   He calls on us continually!

F.   You must say, more or less: we're impotent, we're too exhausted.

M.   But then he becomes violent!

T.   "We can't; please forgive us."

M.   Really abandon him. [softly, as a comment to herself]

F.   But what if he says come, lift the toilet cover for me . . .

M.   [interrupting] Otherwise he won't do his things . . .

F.   . . . The toilet, the toilet cover.

T.   Such minimal things . . .

F.   Yes, minimal . . .

T.   But the important thing is to avoid protecting him.

T. Accepts the Parents' Behavior, but Gives it a Connotation of "Minimal" Help: Reframing and Limitation

T.   Protecting him. Actions . . . above all, not spying on him, absolutely not?!

T.   Very well.

F.   But besides . . .

T.   [interrupting] Only those little things.

F.   That, one might say, is the level of our behavior.

T.   Very good.

M.   Doctor, sometimes he puts his hands on me.

T.   What?

M.   He touches my breasts sometimes. And he has also walked naked . . .

T.   Hmm.

M.   Yes, in the past.

T.   Let's look at the present now. If he touches your breasts—what would a mother do to a son who touches her breasts?

M.   Er. . . [she makes a gesture; the words don't come to her]

T.   She gives him a good slap.

M.   Then he will slap me back, Doctor! What can I do when I'm alone in the house?

T.   Tell his father.

M.   And when my husband isn't there, where do I go and fetch him?

T.   You scold him. O.K.?

M.   He gets violent, Doctor.

T.   All right, Mrs. . . .

M.   I get scared when he is violent, Doctor.

T.   Right. Well. You are right.

F.   [intervening quickly, he turns toward his wife—this is something quite rare: during the first session the two have addressed the therapist in a parallel position to each other, even when they were communicating with each other] Let's listen to the doctor!

T.   But cases like these, the victims are the worst. Right?

M.   Yes.

T.   You know, I always say that persecutors exist because there are victims, and not the other way around. Those who take the role of victim make others into their persecutors. All right? So let's not assume these positions. All right?

F.   You don't think we should ask B. "what did you do, what did you say to the doctor?"

T.   No. Agreed?

SECOND SESSION

The patient returned saying that the past week had been better, because he hadn't vomited very much.

T.   How many times did you do it?

P.   Actually, they decreased.

T.   By how much?

P.   By a lot; one day this week I vomited five, six times, but after that . . . only twice yesterday, for example, and not even once the first day.

T.   Was there any improvement?

P.   Yes, something did improve because of what I was supposed to think about . . . about the positive thing . . .

T.   What is the positive usefulness of your symptoms? Did you discover it?

P.   I often repeated to myself: "A good thing, a good thing because it's keeping my family together."

T.   What effect did that have on you?

P.   I don't know.

T.   Did you feel important?

P.   Yes, yes.

T.   Good. Your symptoms have decreased; and what effect does this fact have on you?

P.   I don't know . . . I've considered that maybe the fact of being important . . . I was important to my family with my fixations; I felt that this was like a prevention of the symptoms. It had a good effect on me, in any case; I don't know . . .

T.   Hmm. And how has your family reacted to the fact that your symptoms have diminished? Do they know?

P.   Yes, they know. Nothing in particular.

The reframing about the usefulness of his symptoms as a sacrifice to his family had the usual effect of decreasing them. Referring to the half-hour paradoxical prescription, he said that, as also usually happens, he did not become anxious or terrified by his obsessive thoughts. So I started the session with a redefinition of this first change and its effects on the patient and his family. Then I prescribed that he "avoid avoiding," because this would be another important contribution to his family's balance (paradoxical prescription). I again prescribed the half-hour "worst fantasy" ritual and, in addition, a direct counterritual:

T.   You must do exactly what I'm about to tell you. From now until we meet again, each time that you feel like doing your washings, or vomiting, or performing all the possible rituals to purify yourself, to cleanse yourself of contamination . . . all the things you might think of doing, so the alcohol, the lips, the splashing, the vomiting . . . your sex . . . you must do it ten times, no more, no less. Exactly ten times, no less, no more, all right? So don't forget: every time that you happen to perform one of your washings or rituals, you must repeat it ten times, not once more nor once less . . .

    P.   Vomiting?

    T.   Yes, exactly ten times, not once more nor once less . . .

    P.   That's hard . . .

    T.   Yes, but the best way to come out of it is to go right through it . . . just imagine . . . you are standing with your feet on hot coal; you are burning yourself; if you don't move, you'll burn more and more; I am trying to make you run, but clearly you will have to burn yourself a little. So, every time you feel like performing your rituals, whether it is washing yourself with alcohol or vomiting, whether it is using disinfection anywhere, you must repeat what you do exactly ten times, not once more nor once less, every time you do something to disinfect yourself, O.K.? Then you will tell me all about it.

After meeting with the boy, I met with his parents, reinforcing their collaboration (which was to consist of avoiding interfering with their son's behavior). I was very careful not to fall into the trap of working on their problems as a couple at this time although the wife repeatedly asked for this, because that kind of shift would have undermined the work that focused on solving their son's problem.

THIRD SESSION

The patient reported a further decrease of symptoms, so I started to investigate his relationships outside the family.

    T.   But, what about girls? Do you still watch them or are you afraid they might approach you, because of the problems we're having?

    P.   No, no, I do watch them . . .

    T.   You aren't afraid they might infect . . .

    P.   Yes, O.K. But it's been a long time since I kissed a girl; I haven't been well in my leg . . .

    T.   Would you like to?

P.   Yes.

Anticipating the   T.   But are you afraid . . . you know . . . that if you
Patient's Thoughts   kiss them they might infect you with all your
                                     things . . . ?

P.   Yes. Yes.

T.   You have that fear?

P.   Yes.

Then I asked about the effects of the prescriptions. He reported that during the half-hour task he had again not felt anxious.

P.   I'm better where my fixations are concerned,
        because they have become less intense. But I feel
        very irritated . . .

T.   With what?

P.   With myself.

T.   Well, how many times did you wash yourself in
        this period of time?

P.   I did the ten times . . .

T.   Good; what happened when you repeated ten
        times, not once more nor once less?

P.   I repeated ten times.

T.   Always exactly ten times?

P.   Yes.

T.   Always exactly ten times . . . neither once more
        nor once less . . . once you got to the tenth, that
        was enough . . . did you stop earlier sometimes?

P.   Sometimes. No, only when I vomited.

T.   Ten times, is that hard? [smiling]

P.   Yes, yes.

T.   Good; most times you did it ten times, and then
        you stopped. Good. I told you to do it ten times,
        not once more nor once less, and you did it ten
        times and then stopped. What does this make
        you think?

P.   I don't know, I can't say.

T.   Don't you think you're beginning to take pos-
        session of your symptoms, and a little more
        power to manage them?

P. Er . . . yes, maybe, but I'm still very undecided about my things.

Paradoxical Reframing T. Sure, if we can't reduce a symptom by trying to
of the Symptoms   reduce it, then we must learn to control it by provoking it. Therefore, in dealing with symptoms and rituals such as yours, the more one tries not to do them, the more one ends up doing them. The more one tries to make them stay put, the more they come out. It's like trying to keep a cat in a bag—the more you try to hold it inside, the more it will scratch, and in the end it will break the bag and jump out. Now, that's what you do with your symptoms. What I am trying to teach you is that you can master your symptoms and gain power over them by provoking them more. Just as you can do them more, you can also do them less—much less.

After these redefinitions I again prescribed the same tasks, only increasing the ritual of the worst fantasy to forty minutes. Then I received the parents; as usual with this kind of family, they started by focusing on the bad attitudes of their son, and only later paid any attention to the observed change.

T. Well, have you noticed any improvements?

F. Well, I say yes . . .

Emphasizing the   T. What have you noticed?
Changes Obtained F. Since he came here the first time, he started to do without the vomiting for two days; then he started again, but much less nervously, almost just for the sake of doing it.

T. He's told me that he does it that certain number of times, but without . . .

F. Yes, yes. Just for the sake of doing it; before, there were times when he threw up everything he had eaten—

M. But he never dries himself when he does his cleanings, and he gets up in the morning and doesn't wash his face.

T. Let your husband finish.

F. I was only saying that, on the whole, he seems much more compliant, apart from the episode on Saturday because then he was stung in something that is particularly important to him; I explained why it's better to wait, but of course he didn't care too much about my reasons. He didn't take up the subject much again, so in general I've noticed some improvement, together with this state of . . . excessive calmness.

After some redefinitions of the evolving situation, I reinforced the parents' task.

Renewing the Prescription for the Parents to Act as Cotherapists

T. Therefore, since you are very good at this, I want to ask you to observe the things I am making him do, without intervening. Nobody else can do them for him. All right?

M. But sometimes he's the one who gets the most angry. I don't. I am more resigned . . .

F. But not in these things. Sometimes I say, "But what are you looking for, you know there's nothing there"; it just slips out of my mouth.

T. You mustn't say that to him. You must only observe. "Just look around, look around. Go ahead and look for it."

F. Oh, but I did that the other day: " Here's a little broom," I told him. "While you're looking around anyway, you can sweep a bit; there's a lot of scrap paper lying around."

T. Good. Let me go ahead. You observe. And be so good as to only observe. All right? Then you will report to me about what's happening.

FOURTH SESSION

T. Tell me what you've been up to this week.

P. Doctor, I took the liberty of keeping a log of how many times I vomited.

T.   Good; you've made an inventory.

P.   Practically, I made myself vomit a total of six times.

T.   By how much have you decreased, then?

P.   Quite a bit.

T.   How much is that?

P.   A lot, I think—because before, it was much more. I also suffered a minor crisis, because on Monday, on the way back from I.—because I spent the weekend in I.—on the way home I noticed a small mark on my foot and imagined that I had been pierced by needle, so I took some peroxide, and rubbed so much with the cotton wool that I wore my skin off, and destroyed my foot.

T.   Not bad.

P.   I destroyed my foot. I also wanted to tell you— last week I forgot to tell you—that while I was walking in my aunt's park I suddenly felt a sharp object near my leg. Then I went home and started thinking about it, and in the end I actually decided to go back to the same place, just to check.

T.   To the scene of the crime.

P.   To check if there was a needle or anything like that on the ground, and look at the mark on my foot. And last night I had to go back to the same street again.

T.   To the scene of the crime.

P.   To the scene of the crime.

T.   To see if you can find something?

P.   Yes.

T.   And you won't be happy until you find something.

P.   No, I don't have to find anything.

T.   You've got to. You've got to find something. Why would you be looking for it, if you didn't have to find it?

P.   No, on the contrary—I have to go there to assure myself that I won't find anything to make sure there's nothing there.

Further Remarks on the
Paradoxical Functioning
of His Perceptive-
Reactive System

T. Yeah, well . . . anyway, your symptoms have decreased.

P. Oh, yes. I feel better. And I went to I. on Saturday and Sunday; I went to the disco.

T. Really!

P. No. Yes. I had fun, I had a few drinks. I shouldn't. I got a bit drunk, let's say.

T. That's all we needed. Were you alone, or with your friends?

P. With my friends, a lot of friends.

T. And were there any girls?

P. Yes, but I didn't make any contact. Quite the opposite. But . . . I want to have a relationship with a girl, because I'm tired of being alone.

T. Did you carry out the tasks I gave you last time?

P. The one about the ten times? When I vomited, I never said the "ten times" task, but I did it when I washed my hands, and with the bidet.

T. And what effect did that have?

P. I don't know, I can't say. I got tired of doing it ten times.

T. Ten times is quite a lot.

P. Yes.

T. So, apart from the vomiting, were the other symptoms more or less frequent than usual?

P. Less frequent. One thing that I often worry about is the idea of being pricked by a needle.

The patient showed a real decrease of obsessive rituals and a return to social life, accompanied by the desire, which had been blocked by the fear of contagion, to continue a relationship with a girl. But parallel to this improvement a new phobic fixation appeared: a sort of hallucination of feeling needles puncturing him while walking in the streets. The session with him ended with the assignment of homework: the previous prescription was maintained; paradoxically I warned him not to touch a girl because it would be very dangerous.

Prescription of Another
Paradoxical Ritual

T. Every time you go out alone, and start feeling those imaginary needles, I want you to take your needle and prick your left hand with your right, five times, and your right hand with your left, five times. Then you put the needle back in its place.

P. Er . . . I have to take a needle, and every time I become fixated on feeling that something's pricking me, I have to prick my right hand five times and my left hand five times.

T. Every time you feel those injection needles piercing you. For example, this evening, if you want to go and see the famous needle place because you're afraid that you may been pricked by a needle, you take your own needle along, go to that place and . . . prick, prick, prick, prick, prick. You don't have to push too hard—just feel a slight little pain.

P. Without making it bleed.

T. That's obvious. All right?

P. I understand.

T. Every time, from now until next week, O.K.?

P. O.K.

T. Each task is stranger than the other. But as you have seen, these things work. Are you satisfied or not with the way things have been going until now?

P. Yes, but I would like to got to the point that I would want to clean the blood off the injection needle, by myself; I already said that last time.

T. Of course. You'll get there.

Next I met with the parents. Together we evaluated the actual results and then I reinforced their therapeutic collaboration of observing without intervening.

FIFTH SESSION

Asking about the Changes that have Occurred during the Week

T. What's happening? From your telephone call, it seemed that there were some good things going on.

P. Yes. I feel well.

T. What do you mean, you "feel well"?

P. I even kissed a girl. Not one of those passionate kisses . . .

T. What was it like?

P. A kiss on the mouth. I would have, but I didn't like the girl, so . . .

T. So why did you kiss her?

P. Maybe because . . . I hadn't kissed a girl for a long time.

T. And where did it happen? Tell me about it.

P. I'm going back to I. again tomorrow. I go to the disco at least three times a week now.

T. Do you enjoy it?

P. Yes, I do; apart from the fact that my leg is still hurting a bit. I also went back to that place, as you told me. I did find a syringe, but it was ugly, without a needle or anything.

T. How could it have stuck you, otherwise?

P. Then I had a suspicion, and found a little spot just above my foot, and started asking myself whether I might have pricked myself by accident, and when I had that suspicion, and had the tests made, and called you.

T. Was there anything wrong?

P. No, nothing.

T. Good. Did you continue playing the little game of pricking yourself with the needles?

P. Yes. I keep my pins here.

T. Good. What was the effect of playing that little game?

P. No particular effect.

T. Did you still see needles pricking you? How many times did you see them? Or feel them?

P. No, very few times this week, actually. But one thing happened that upset me, because I didn't feel any pain; I only remember spraining my leg on the street where I found the syringe.

T. And how many times did you have to prick yourself with the needles?

P. Twice.

T.   Show me the needles you've chosen.

P.   No, they're pins.

T.   Very well, pins. You've sterilized them, haven't you?

P.   No. I bought them new.

T.   Well, good. And how many times did you prick yourself? Twice? Ten times?

P.   Five times on this hand and five on the other.

T.   Good. Did you feel any pain?

P.   A little.

T.   And what was the effect when you did it?

P.   Oh, I don't know. Maybe a feeling of pain.

T.   And you only did it twice?

P.   Maybe it's the beneficial effect of dispelling the doubt . . . the doubt that I might be HIV-positive . . . from having pricked myself . . . because it's very difficult to become HIV-positive by pricking oneself with a needle.

T.   And what about all the other rituals?

P.   No, nothing. I only vomited three times.

T.   Only three times in the whole week?

P.   Yes, although I did sporadically. No crises. I'm well. I feel good.

T.   How do you explain this improvement?

P.   I don't know.

T.   How much do you think you have improved?

P.   By 20 percent.

T.   What do you mean? That we've reduced your problems by 20 percent?

P.   By yet another 20 percent.

T.   So where are we now?

P.   At well over 50 percent, I think.

T.   We've resolved more than half. About 50 or 60 percent?

P.   Yes. Oh, and I felt quite ready to wipe the blood off my mother. I didn't do it, but I felt ready. I mean, I could have done it.

After these developments, I proceeded to redefine what had happened at a cognitive level. His contact with the girl was seen as the most significant development. The therapy could thus evolve into the patient's gradual exposition to all the situations he perceived as fearful, with the possibility of performing my counterrituals instead of the original obsessive compulsions.

T.   Well, well. Now, this week we must do even more, but slowly, very slowly; we mustn't go too fast. Slowly. So keep on doing everything you spontaneously feel like doing—going out with other people, having fun, kissing. It's nice to kiss. And do some other things too, because that's even nicer. Continue to take those pins along, and every time you feel that you're being pricked [gestures]: five times and five times. All right? As for the ritual of washing yourself with alcohol and so on, from now until next week, every day. I'd like you to halt that famous half hour. But in that half hour, you'll be doing some other things. You will go about the house for half an hour every day, and touch all the things that you consider most contaminated, the toilet . . . certain things that you consider most contaminated.

P.   I have to touch them.

Desensitizing
Paradoxical
Prescription

T.   You have to touch them. And after that, you will wash your hands exactly ten times; wash them and dry them ten times. You wash them and dry them ten times. All that, for half an hour every day. So instead of thinking about the worst during that half hour, you do the worst. Is that clear?

P.   Yes.

T.   So what do you imagine that you will do?

P.   I touch the toilet, the bidet, my mother's towel.

T.   And then? You must get dirty, contaminate yourself, and then wash yourself—wash yourself each time—within half an hour every day.

P.   Do you mean that I should touch things for half an hour and then wash myself at the end?

T.   Either that, or touch and wash, touch and wash, within that half-hour, whichever you prefer.

P.   O.K.

T. And always carry the pins with you because they must accompany you everywhere, and every time you feel that you're being pricked, you prick yourself with the pins.

P. Doctor, how can I get rid of the doubt . . . with the pins?

T. You prick yourself with the pins. Every time you have the doubt, you prick yourself with the pins. And let's see if you really manage to get together with that girl.

P. Tomorrow.

T. I don't think you'll make it. What do you say?

P. I think I will.

T. I think you won't.

P. Let's make a bet.

T. Yes, let's make a bet. And let's go slow, don't hurry too much, avoid avoiding, but don't go too fast, don't expect yourself to wipe your mother's blood off the injection needle, but do exchange things with her. All right. Now I'm going to speak with your parents.

The parents declared that the situation had further improved, but as usual in these cases, they began to complain about their son's bad manners. From "mad to bad" is a common progression in these kinds of families, because the parents need their son's problem in order to survive as a couple (if their son did not have a problem to fight, they would start fighting between themselves). However, I redefined the results with them without accepting any shift in the goals of the therapy.

SIXTH SESSION

The patient reported a slight improvement in his ability to expose himself to previous contagious-laden objects at home, without the need to make any obsessive rituals. He also continued to meet the girl and kiss her, feeling no fear of contagion. So the therapy evolved forward, with my suggestions of counterrituals to counteract his fear of contagious-laden situations. For the first time the parents did not come to the session.

SEVENTH SESSION

Weekly Report

T. How many times did you splash in the water?

P. I vomited. I vomited five times. But I've come a great step forward, because I've kissed her; and she had a herpes blister here [he points to his lips], so I vomited five times.

T. Did you do anything more? Did you wash with alcohol?

P. The penis a little, with alcohol, once.

T. How did you manage with the tasks?

P. I was supposed to prick myself with the pins and go looking for needles. But I didn't, also because it rained. But I did some therapy: there was a needle on the table; I picked it up and pricked myself, instead of going on site.

T. Now, what about that girl? Did you make it with her, or not?

P. I did, yes.

T. Tell me how you spend your days now.

P. I spend them together with the girl, kissing and talking with our friends.

In addition, he reported that he had stopped using alcohol to clean his body, only using it when vomiting. He had also been able to expose himself, in a natural manner, to many situations that he would have previously considered contagious.

T. Good, good. By what percentage have we improved now?

P. Since the beginning?

T. Yes, since the beginning.

P. Well, about 60, 68 percent.

T. Not bad. Hmm.

I redefined the changes that had occurred within the family relationships and ended the session by repeating the previous prescription of exposing himself to further fear-laden situations. The parents did not come again.

EIGHTH SESSION (AFTER THREE WEEKS)

Renewing the Prescription and Encouraging the Patient's Experiences with the Girl. Report.

T.   Hello. So how is it going? How are you feeling?

P.   Quite well.

T.   Good. How are things going?

P.   I'm doing all right as far as my fixations are concerned. It's been a long time now since our last meeting. I'm doing O.K. I've vomited three or four times. Then, the most important thing is that I don't really feel like talking about these things.

After reporting these results, he introduced the problems that had arisen from his desire to move to the island of Ischia for the summer together with the girl. The problems were his mother's reactions and the crisis between his parents, which eventually led to their separation. So we talked a lot about his parents' problems and about the role that his disease had played in keeping the couple united.

T.   But your parents . . . just think, until a few months ago, your family was accustomed to having a son with an enormous problem. Now things have changed so much that your family has to find a new balance.

P.   Oh, yes, that's true.

Then he reported a problem with the girl: she wanted to make love but he was afraid to. So the therapy evolved toward the solution of this small but significant problem.

Prescribing a Final Ritual

T.   I think that since you want to do it, you must prepare the whole thing well. In the next few days, you'll have to construct some ideal situations for yourself. I leave you the choice of using a condom or not; but you'll have to give her a surprise, and find an isolated place where you can feel at ease, and where you could do it. Where would you like to do it?

P.   Oh, I don't know.

T. Outside? On the beach?

P. Oh, yes, on the beach.

T. Have you already started swimming, or not?

P. No, I haven't. I haven't been into the sea yet, but a friend told me the water is cold, very cold.

T. Very, very cold? Good.

P. The weather hasn't been very good.

T. [very slowly] You go to the beach [pause]. You choose whether or not to use a condom. You bring the situation up to a certain point. You consummate, and then . . . immediately afterward . . . immediately afterward, you take your socks take your trousers off, take your T-shirt off; take everything off and plunge into the cold water.

P. No, [very perplexed] I have to make love with her . . . and then bathe in the cold water!? Is that what I have to do?

T. Yes! All right? You can even do it more than once. An far as I'm concerned, it's enough that you do it just once.

P. And what if I don't make love to her in the next fifteen days?

T. We'll see if you don't.

P. What bothers me is that I think I have to disinfect myself with alcohol afterward.

T. There's sea water, isn't there? It's . . . cold.

P. So that's my task?

T. You must go to the beach, and be particularly slow in bringing her . . . in building up . . . you must get very excited and then . . . when you have consummated all . . . like certain monks used to do, when they consummated their sexual relationships and had to punish themselves, they used to dive into icy water and punish themselves with icy water.

P. And what if I do it at home, what do I do then? Do I still have to go swimming?

T. Of course. Off you go to the beach and into the cold water; you have to punish yourself.

NINTH SESSION

T. Did you have a good trip?

P. Yes. The sun is shining.

T. So how are things going for you?

P. Oh, I'm doing all right. I'm doing well. Very well, actually.

T. What does "very well" mean?

P. I called you once, but then I stopped worrying. It was because I had stained myself with blood, but I calmed down because I remembered that there had been no problems last time it happened.

T. And what about the rest . . .

P. I did it. I did it on the beach. Oh, how I swore! It was incredibly, incredibly cold. I'll never forget it. It was just too horrible; the water was freezing, the evening was cold . . .

T. Tell me everything, from A to Z. I gave you a specific prescription, and what did you do?

P. Let's say . . . we went to the beach. But I did it with a condom.

T. Of course!

P. Why of course?

T. That's good, isn't it? That way you avoid both risks. There's the other risk, of pregnancy.

P. It wasn't all that nice the first time. Neither of us is very experienced, so it was embarrassing, but it went O.K. I dived into the sea afterward, and I tell you, it was incredible. Anyway, I wanted to do it without a condom.

Redefining the   T. The water was cold.
Concluding Ritual

P. Incredibly so—it was freezing.

T. Weren't you afraid that you might have been contaminated?

P. No, but I went home and disinfected myself as usual, and then we did it again.

T. And then you dived into the sea again.

P. No.

T. You didn't dive it again? Just once?

P. No. I feel calm. I thought you might ask me the usual question about how much I have improved. Oh, I've improved more than 85 percent.

Evaluation and
Redefinition of the
Changes Obtained

T. Do you have to purify yourself every time you do it with her?

P. Just my penis.

T. Any other kinds of purification?

P. No, no.

T. You haven't vomited anymore?

P. No, except for a couple of times in the past fifteen days, because there were certain circumstances. For example, because I had kissed her while there was a little blood running out of her mouth. And then she stupidly licked me on the mouth. But only in those kinds of circumstances. I don't think I'm going to vomit anymore; that's almost over.

T. Do you think about the past, once in a while?

P. No.

Then we talked about the beach ritual, laughing over it and evaluating how this was also a real improvement over his previous impairing fixations. After that he explained how he found a job to be able to stay on the island of I. Together we considered the relationship of his personal independence to his personal balance, and how it was also a step toward the complete solution of the problem. I ended the session without any prescriptions, and met with the patient's father.

T. Well, it seems to me that things are still going the best possible way.

F. Yes, I think so. I suppose so. But unfortunately, there's one thing . . . which by now . . . He has improved considerably, no doubt, but he just can't wait; he doesn't know what he wants to do, and as a result he ends up doing what he wants all the time. Last night he wanted to come with me to N. I told him we were going to leave at six. When I came home, he had called to say he wasn't coming. He tries to take advantage of favorable opportunities to break loose. I understand him, and I am more indulgent, but he wants all sorts of impossible things and, as if it weren't enough, he blames me.

T. Yes, but you must realize that . . .

P. I do realize it. I'm astonished by the results, but he's poisoning our existence; he always has to make problems for us; he can't live without problems.

Encouraging the Parents to be Independent Now that They Are Free of the Problem

T. You must think about your own problems now: your wife, your work, your things. I'll take care of B. All that you need to do is collaborate. B. has mentioned a series of projects: going to university, finishing a two-year academic program in one year. All he needs is some guidance.

TENTH SESSION

Redefining the Results

T. What have you got to tell me?

P.   Everything is going well. Nothing special.

T. Is everything going well? You haven't had any more of those problems?

P. No. I don't vomit anymore, so I don't know what to say. Everything is going well.

T. Everything is going well; your problems are nothing more than an old memory. Good!

P. I've reached a good percentage. The only obstacle left is toward making love without a condom.

T. And did we continue bathing in the sea?

P. Oh, yes, yes.

T. So, what do you do when you make love after going swimming?

P. I go to the bathroom and wash only that part.

T. And does she wash herself?

P. Yes.

T. Oh! You both wash . . . hmm . . . so the only

problem left is doing it with her, without a condom.

P.   And apart from that, I have no problems, because the other day a pimple on a friend of mine started bleeding; he got his hands all dirty when he wiped it off, and I touched his hands and didn't worry about it.

T.   What about the needles pricking you?

P.   I'm slightly more careful on the beach, but that's normal.

T.   And have you come across any more needles that were, and weren't, there?

P.   No.

T.   Good. And what is happening with your parents?

P.   My period of confusion is starting to come to an end. I'm happy that the old problems are gone; there are some new problems. I don't know. My mother isn't very happy; she isn't making a lot of money on her job, and it's especially important to make money right now, so that we can go and live at I. We've found a new house, a villa, but what we need is money.

T.   And are you working?

P.   I had a job for a few days, but I haven't found a steady job.

T.   Didn't you have a job driving around making deliveries?

P.   Oh, yes. But you need a driver's license for that. I haven't got one—I'm not 18 yet. I have to look around for a part-time job; then, in September I'm going to start studying again.

T.   And have an important profession when you grow up.

P.   I hope so.

T.   So none of your fixations or rituals have shown up again . . . you've done no more of that.

P.   No, no.

The Patient Gets the   T.   The credit is yours, much more than mine. You
Credit for the Change   had the resources; all I did was prompt you. I

didn't put in anything that you didn't already have within. All I did was stimulate your resources to make them come out. My task was no more than that. You have the responsibility for such a speedy, important change. I had to play a few of those rather strange, funny games.

P.   Too strange, even.

T.   Too strange, even because I had to stimulate your resources that way—by asking you to do things that way. You wouldn't have done it without those little games. This way, instead, you have recovered your personal resources.

T.   As far as I'm concerned, B., the therapy is finished. I will only be checking up on the results.

P.   Oh, is it already finished?

T.   It's only a matter of arranging things so that you can go ahead, but enthusiastically.

P.   So it's all up to me? . . . Doctor, I would like another favor. At the time, my mother promised me that as soon as I was well again my maternal grandmother would give me a motorcycle. I have always wanted a motorcycle. If you could . . . I don't know . . . give me a piece of paper that says I have recovered now.

T.   In September.

P.   In September? O.K.

Epilogue: Caveats

As with all therapeutic prescriptions that are worthy of respect, ours too should bear its caveats.

The kind of treatment that has been presented here is inadvisable for those patients who feel that the therapist should be their confessor and comforter, or that the therapist's main task is to offer them absolute and reassuring "truths" to believe in. Moreover, this treatment is decidedly inappropriate for those who are looking for a figure with whom to establish a long, intense, and passionate therapeutic relationship.

Finally, this treatment is not recommended for those who wish to set out on that fascinating journey within the mysteries of their psyches, in quest of their true selves (revealed and expounded on by the latest psychoanalyst).

All these types of patients are cautioned to carefully avoid therapists that are able to carry out the kind of treatment described in this book, because our experience has shown that a certain degree of "addiction" tends to occur.

In other words, it has been observed that quick and effective solutions to the deep and sad problems of the above-mentioned patients can lead to sensible alterations in these patients' ways of perceiving and evaluating issues to the point of changing their mind on what the "right" therapy should be.

I would like to add a fantasy of mine. Based on my own experience, also shared by my colleagues at the Mental Research Institute, I am almost sure that the author of this book will be called a "manipulator." This so modern (or maybe even postmodern?), accusation prompts the following question (which, so far, none of my colleagues has been able to answer): Is it possible to imagine an act of help that is not manipulative? To help means to exercise influences over another. If I jump into the water to save someone who is about to drown, am I manipulating him?

Paul Watzlawick

References

American Psychiatric Association (1994). *Diagnostic and Statistical Manual of Mental Disorders,* 4th ed. Washington, DC: American Psychiatric Association.

Amerio, P. (1982). *Teorie in Psicologia Sociale (Social Psychology Theories)*. Bologna: Il Mulino.

Andolfi, M. (1991). Tre generazioni in terapia (Three generations in therapy). In *Dall'Individuo al Sistema (From Individual to System)*, ed. M. Malagoli-Togliatti and U. Telfener, pp. 38–51. Torino: Boringhieri.

Andrews, G., and Harvey, R. (1981). Does psychotherapy benefit neurotic patients? A reanalysis of the Smith, Glass and Miller data. *Archives of General Psychiatry* 38:1203–1208.

Anonymous (1991). *I 36 Stratagemmi (The 36 Strategems)*. Naples: Guida.

Ashby, W. R. (1954). *Design for a Brain*. New York: Wiley.

——— (1956). *An Introduction to Cybernetics*. London: Methuen.

Austin, J. L. (1962). *How to Do Things with Words*. Cambridge, MA: Harvard University Press.

Avnet, H. H. (1965). How effective is short-term therapy? In *Short-Term Psychotherapy*, ed. L. R. Wolberg. New York: Grune & Stratton.

Bandler, R., and Grinder, J. (1975a). *Patterns of the Hypnotic Technique of Milton J. Erickson, M.D.* Palo Alto, CA: Meta.

——— (1975b). *The Structure of Magic*. Palo Alto, CA: Meta.

Bandura, A. (1974). *Psychological Modeling*. Chicago: Aldine.

———— (1977). *Social Learning Theory*. Englewood Cliffs, NJ: Prentice-Hall.

Bannister, D., and Fransella, F. (1977). *Inquiring Man: The Theory of Personal Constructs*. Harmondsworth, England: Penguin.

Bateson, G. (1967). Cybernetic Explanation. *American Behavioral Scientist* 10:29–32.

———— (1972). *Steps to an Ecology of Mind*. New York: Ballantine.

———— (1979). *Mind and Nature*. New York: Bantam.

Bateson, G., and Jackson, D. D. (1964). Some varieties of pathogenic organization. *Disorders of Communication* (Research Publications, Association for Research in Nervous and Mental Disease) 42:270–283.

Bateson, G., Jackson, D. D., Haley, J., and Weakland, J. H. (1956). Toward a theory of schizophrenia. *Behavioral Sciences* 1:261–264.

Beck, A. T., and Emery, G. (1985). *Anxiety Disorders and Phobia*. New York: Basic Books.

Bergin, A. E., and Lambert, M. J. (1978). The evaluation of therapeutic outcomes. In *Handbook of Psychotherapy and Behavior Change*, ed. S. L. Garfield and A. E. Bergin, 2nd ed. New York: Wiley.

Bergin, A. E., and Strupp, H. H. (1972). *Changing Frontiers in the Science of Psychotherapy*. Chicago: Aldine.

Bergman, J. S. (1985). *Fishing for Barracuda: Pragmatics of Brief Systemic Therapy*. New York: Norton.

Birdwhistel, R. (1970). Metacommunicational thoughts: about communication studies. In *A Language*, ed. R. Jakin et al. The Hague: Molton.

Bloch, A. (1989). *La Legge di Murphy e Altri Motivi per Cui le Cose Vanno a Rovescia*. Milan: Longanesi.

Bodin, A. (1980). The interactional view: family therapy approaches of the Mental Research Institute. In *The Handbook of Family Therapy*, ed. A. S. Gurman and D. P. Kniskern. New York: Brunner/Mazel.

Boscolo, L., Cecchin, G., Hoffman, L., and Penn, P. (1988). *Milan Systemic Family Therapy*. New York: Basic Books.

Bourn, E. J. (1990). *The Anxiety and Phobia Workbook*. Oakland, CA: New Harlinger.

Brown, G. S. (1973). *Laws of Form*. New York: Bantam.

Butcher, J. N., and Koss, M. P. (1978). M.M.P.I. research on brief and crisis-oriented therapies. In *Handbook of Psychotherapy and Behavior Change*, ed. S. L. Garfield and A. E. Bergin, 2nd ed. New York: Wiley.

Cancrini, L. (1987). *Psicoterapia: Sintassi e Grammatica* (*Psychotherapy: Syntax and Grammar*). Rome: La Nuova Italia.

Cecchin, G. F. (1990). Personal communication, at the fear, phobia, panic: models of treatment panel. The International Congress, April, Arezzo.

Ceronetti, G. (1987). *Pensieri de Te* (*Teatime Thinking*). Milan: Adelphi.

Chambers, G. S., and Hamlin, R. (1957). The validity of judgments based on "blind" Rorschach records. *Journal of Consulting Psychology* 21:105–109.

Cialdini, R. B. (1984). *How and Why People Agree to Things.* New York: William Morrow.

de Shazer, S. (1982). *Patterns of Brief Therapy.* New York: Guilford.

————— (1985). *Keys to Solution in Brief Therapy.* New York: Norton.

————— (1991). *Putting Difference to Work.* New York: Norton.

————— (1994). *Words Were Originally Magic.* New York: Norton.

Eigen, M. (1986). *Il Gioco.* Milan: Adelphi.

Ellis, A. (1981). Teoria e prassi della RET (Theory and practice of Rational Emotive Therapy). In *Cognitivismo e Psicoterapia,* ed. Guidano and Reda. Milan: Angeli.

Elster, J. (1979). *Ulysses and the Sirens.* Cambridge, England: Cambridge University Press.

Erickson, M. H., and Rossi, E. L., eds. (1982). *The Collected Papers of Milton H. Erickson on Hypnosis.* New York: Irvington.

Erickson, M. H., Rossi, E. L., and Rossi, S. I. (1979). *Hypnotic Realities: The Induction of Clinical Hypnosis and Forms of Indirect Suggestion.* New York: Irvington.

Fisch, R., Watzlawick, P., Weakland, J. H., and Bodin, A. (1982a). On unbecoming family therapists. In *The Book of Family Therapy,* ed. A. Ferber, M. Mendelson, and A. Napier. New York: Science House.

Fisch, R., Weakland, J. H., Watzlawick, P., et al. (1975). *Learning Brief Therapy: An Introductory Training Manual.* Palo Alto, CA: Mental Research Institute.

Fisch, R., Weakland, J. H., and Segal, L. (1982b). *The Tactics of Change.* San Francisco: Jossey-Bass.

Foerster, H. von (1970). Thoughts and notes on cognition. In *Cognition: A Multiple View,* ed. P. L. Garvin, pp. 25–48. New York: Plenum.

————— (1973). On constructing reality. In *Environmental Design Research,* ed. F. E. Preiser, pp. 35–46. Stroudsburg, PA: Douden, Hutchinson, and Ross. (Reprinted in Watzlawick 1984.)

————— (1974). Kybernetik einer erkennthistorie (Cybernetic epistemology). In *Kybernetik und Bionik* (*Cybernetics and Bionics*), ed. W. D. Keidel, W. Handler, and M. Spring. Munich: Oldenburg.

————— (1981). *Observing Systems.* Seaside, CA: Intersystems (this is the English ed. of Foerster 1977).

————— (1984). On constructing a reality. In *The Invented Reality,* ed. P. Watzlawick. New York: Norton.

————— (1987). *Sistemi Che si Osservano.* Rome: Astrolabio.

Frank, J. D. (1971). Therapeutic components of psychotherapy. A 25-year progress report of research. *Journal of Consulting and Clinical Psychology* 37:307–313.

Frankl, V. E. (1960). Paradoxical intention. *American Journal of Psychotherapy* 14:520–535.

Galli, P. G., ed. (1987). *Lewin: Written Anthology.* Bologna: Il Mulino.

Garfield, S. L. (1980). *Psychotherapy: an Eclectic Approach.* New York: Wiley.

———— (1981). Psychotherapy: a 40-year appraisal. *American Psychologist* 2:174–183.

———— (1989). *The Practice of Brief Psychotherapy.* New York: Pergamon.

Garfield, S. L., Prager, R. A., and Bergin, A. E. (1971). Evaluation of outcome in psychotherapy. *Journal of Consulting and Clinical Psychology* 37:307–313.

Giannattasio, E., and Nencini, R. (1983). *Conoscenza e Modellazione Nella Psicologia (Knowledge and Model-Constructing in Psychology).* Rome: La Goliardica.

Giles, T. R. (1983). Probable superiority of behavioral interventions: I: Traditional comparative outcome. *Journal of Behavior Therapy and Experimental Psychiatry* 14:29–32.

Glasersfeld, E. von (1979). Cybernetic experience and concept of self. In *A Cybernetic Approach to Assessment of Children: Towards More Humane Use of Human Beings,* ed. M. N. Ozer. Boulder, CO: Westview.

———— (1984). An introduction to radical constructivism. In *The Invented Reality,* ed. P. Watzlawick. New York: Norton.

———— (1995). *Radical Constructivism.* Bristol: Falmer.

Goethe, J. W. (1983). *Massime e Riflessioni (Aphorisms and Reflections).* Rome: Theoria.

Goldwurm, G., et al. (1986). *Tecniche di Rilassamento Nella Terapia Comportamentale (Techniques of Relaxation in Behavioral Therapy).* Milan: Angeli.

Gracian, B. (1967). *Oracolo Manuale e Arte di Prudenza (Handy Oracle and Prudence Art).* Milan: Rizzoli.

Greenberg, G. (1980). Problem-focused brief family interactional psychotherapy. In *Group and Family Therapy,* ed. R. Lewis, M. D. Wolberg, L. Marvin, and P. D. Aronson. New York: Brunner/Mazel.

Guastafson, J. P. (1986). *The Complex Secret of Brief Psychotherapy.* New York: Norton.

Guidano, V. (1988). *La Complessita' del Se (The Complexity of Self).* Torino: Boringhieri.

Gurman, A. S., and Kniskern, D. P. (1978). Research on marital and family therapy. In *Handbook of Psychotherapy and Behavior Change,* ed. S. L. Garfield and A. E. Bergin, 2nd ed. New York: Wiley.

Haley, J. (1967). *Advanced Techniques of Hypnosis and Therapy: Selected Papers of Milton J. Erickson, M.D.* New York/London: Grune & Stratton.

———— (1973). *Uncommon Therapy: The Psychiatric Techniques of Milton J. Erickson, M.D.* New York: Norton.

———— (1976). *Problem-Solving Therapy.* San Francisco: Jossey-Bass.

———— (1985). *Conversations with Milton J. Erickson, M.D.* Vol. 1: *Changing Individuals.* Vol. 2: *Changing Couples.* Vol. 3: *Changing Families and Children.* Chicago: Triangle.

Harris, M. R., Kalis, B., and Freeman, E. (1963). Precipitating stress: an approach to brief therapy. *American Journal of Psychotherapy* 17:465–471.

——— (1964). An approach to short-term psychotherapy. *Mind* 2:198–206.

Hecker, J. E., and Thorpe, G. L. (1992). *Agoraphobia and Panic: A Guide to Psychological Treatment.* Boston: Allyn & Bacon.

Herr, J., and Weakland, J. H. (1979). *Counseling Elders and Their Families.* New York: Springer.

Hoffman, L. (1981). *Foundations of Family Therapy.* New York: Basic Books.

Hoffmannstal, H. V. (1980). *Il Libro degli Amici.* Milan: Adelphi.

Keeney, B. (1985). *L'Estetica del Cambiamento (The Aesthetic of Change).* Rome: Astrolabio.

——— (1991). *La Terapia dell'Improvvisazione (The Therapy of Improvisation).* Rome: Astrolabio.

Kelly, G. A. (1955). *The Psychology of Personal Constructs.* New York: Norton.

Kraus, K. (1972). *Detti e Contraddetti (Sayings and Countersayings).* Milan: Adelphi.

Kuhn, T. (1970). *The Structure of Scientific Revolutions.* Chicago: University of Chicago Press.

Laborit, H. (1982). *L'elogio della Fuga.* Milan: Mondadori.

Lankton, S., and Lankton, C. H. (1983). *The Answer Within: A Clinical Framework of Ericksonian Hypnotherapy.* New York: Brunner/Mazel.

Lazarus, A. A. (1989). *The Practice of Multimodal Therapy.* Baltimore: Johns Hopkins University Press.

Lec, S. (1984). *Pensieri Spettinati.* Milan: Bompiani.

Lichtenberg, C. G. (1978). *Das Lichtenberg trost Buchlein.* Vienna, Munich: Meister Verlag.

Liddle, H. A. (1982). Diagnosis and assessment in family therapy: a comparative analysis of six schools of thought. In *Diagnosis and Assessment in Family Therapy*, ed. B. Keeney. Rockville, MD: Aspen.

Lorenzini, R., and Sassaroli, S. (1987). *La Paura della Paura: un Modello Clinico delle Fobie.* Rome: La Nuova Italia.

Luborsky, L., Singer, B., and Luborsky, L. (1975). Comparative studies of psychotherapies: Is it true that everyone has won and all must have prizes? *Archives of General Psychiatry* 132:995–1004.

Madanes, C. (1981). *Strategic Family Therapy.* San Francisco: Jossey-Bass.

——— (1990). *Behind the One-Way Mirror.* San Francisco: Jossey-Bass.

Mahoney, M. J. (1979). *Cognition and Clinical Science.* New York: Plenum.

——— (1991). *Human Change Process.* New York: Basic Books.

Maisondieu, J., and Matayer, L. (1986). *Les Therapies Familiales.* Paris: Press Universitaires de France.

Malagoli-Togliatti, M., and Telfener, U. (1991). *Dall'individuo al Sistema.* Turin: Boringhieri.

Maturana, H. R. (1978). Biology of language: the epistemology of reality. In *Psychology and Biology of Language and Thought*, ed. G. A. Miller and E. Lennberg. New York: Academic Press.

Minguzzi, G. F. (1986). E' possibile valutare i risultati della psicoterapia? (May we evaluate psychotherapy outcomes?) *Il Giornale Italiano di Psicologia* 13(1):7–13.

Montalvo, B., and Haley, J. (1973). In defense of child therapy. *Family Process* 12:227–244.

Morin, E. (1984). *Scienza con Coscienza*. Milan: Franco Angeli.

———— (1986). *La Methode III. La Connaissance de la Connaissance*. Paris: Seuil.

Muench, G. A. (1965). An investigation of the efficacy of time-limited psychotherapy. *Journal of Counseling Psychology* 12:294–299.

Nardone, G., ed. (1988). *Modelli di Psicoterapia a Confronto* (*Models of Psychotherapy in Comparison*). Rome: Il Ventaglio.

———— (1991). *Suggesione—Ristrutturazione—Cambiamento* (*Suggestion, Reframing, Change*). Milan: Giuffre.

Nardone, G., and Watzlawick, P. (1993). *The Art of Change. Strategic Therapy and Hypnotherapy Without Trance*. San Francisco: Jossey-Bass.

Neumann, J. von, and Morgenstern, O. (1944). *Theory of Games and Economic Behavior*. Princeton, NJ: Princeton University Press.

O'Honlon, W. H., and Weiner Davis, M. (1989). *In Search of Solution*. New York: Norton.

———— (1990). *An Uncommon Casebook*. New York: Norton.

Pensifory, R. Z. (1988). *Anxiety, Phobias and Panic*. San Francisco: Life Skills.

Philips, E. L., and Wiener, D. N. (1966). *Short-Term Psychotherapy and Structural Behavior Change*. New York: McGraw-Hill.

Popper, K. R. (1968). *Conjectures and Refutations: The Growth of Scientific Knowledge*. New York: Harper Torch Books.

———— (1972). *Objective Knowledge*. London: Oxford University Press.

———— (1973). *Realism and the Aim of Science*. London: Hutchinson.

Prigogine, I. (1980). *From Being to Becoming*. San Francisco: Freeman.

Rabkin, R. (1977). *Strategic Psychotherapy*. New York: Basic Books.

Reda, M. (1986). *Sistemi Cognitivi Complessi e Psicoterapia*. Rome: La Nuova Italia.

Ritterman, M. (1983). *Using Hypnosis in Family Therapy*. San Francisco: Jossey-Bass.

Rogers, C. (1954). *La Terapia Centrata sul Cliente*. Florence: Giunti. *Client-Centered Therapy*. Boston, MA: Houghton Mifflin, 1951.

Rosen, S. (1982). The values and philosophy of Milton Erickson. In *Ericksonian Approaches to Hypnosis and Psychotherapy*, ed. J. Zeig. New York: Brunner/Mazel.

Rosenthal, R. (1966). *Experimenter Effects in Behavioral Research*. New York: Appleton-Century-Crofts.

Salvini, A. (1988). Theorical pluralism and cognitive pragmatism. In *Pluralismo Teorico e Pragmatismo Conoscitivo in Psicologia della Personalità*, ed. E. Fiora, I. Pedrabissi, and A. Salvini, pp. 1–50. Milan: Giuffre.

———— (1991). La paura è semplicemente un'emozione? *Rivista di Scienze Sessuologiche* 4(1):9–16.

Segal, L. (1980). Focused problem resolution. In *Models of Family Therapy*, ed. E. Tolsen and W. J. Reid. New York: Columbia University Press.

Selvini-Palazzoli, M., Boscolo, L., Cecchin, G., and Prata, G. (1975). *Paradosso e Controparadosso*. Milan: Feltrinelli.

Selvini-Palazzoli, M., Cirillo, S., Selvini, M., and Sorrentino, A. (1989). *Family Games: General Models of Psychotic Processes in the Family*. New York: Norton.

Shlien, J. M. (1957). Time-limited psychotherapy: an experimental investigation of practical values and theoretical implications. *Journal of Counseling Psychology* 4:318–329.

Shopenhaur, A. (1980). *Aforismi sulla Saggezza del Vivere (Aphorisms on Living Wisdom)*. Milan: Longanesi.

Simon, B. F., Stierlin, H., and Wynne, C. L. (1985). *The Language of Family Therapy: A Systemic Vocabulary and Sourcebook*. New York: Family Process.

Sirigatti, S. (1975). Behavior therapy and therapist variables. Vol. I: A-B distinction in the treatment of monophobias. *Bollettino di Psicologia Applicata* 127–139.

––––––– (1988). La ricerca valutativa in psicoterapia: modelli e prospettive (Outcome Research in Psychotherapy: Models and Perspectives). In *Modelli di Psicoterapia a Confronto (Models of Psychotherapy in Comparison)*, ed. G. Nardone. Rome: Il Ventaglio.

Skinner, B. F. (1938). *The Behavior of Organism*. New York: Appleton-Century-Crofts.

––––––– (1974). *About Behaviorism*. New York: Knopf.

Sluzki, C. E., and Donald, C. R. (1979). *Double Bind: The Foundation of the Communicational Approach to the Family*. New York: Grune & Stratton.

Smith, M. L., Glass, G. U., and Miller, T. I. (1980). *The Benefit of Psychotherapy*. Baltimore: Johns Hopkins University Press.

Stolzenberg, G. (1978). *Can an Inquiry into the Foundations of Mathematics Tell Us Anything Interesting About Mind?* New York: Academic Press.

Strupp, H. H., and Hadley, S. W. (1979). Specific vs. nonspecific factors in psychotherapy: a controlled study of outcome. *Archives of General Psychiatry* 36:1125–1136.

Talmom, M. (1990). *Single Session Therapy*. San Francisco: Jossey-Bass.

Thom, R. (1990). *Parabole e Catastrofi (Parables and Catastrophes)*. Milan: Il Saggiatore.

Turner, S. M., and Beidel, D. C. (1988). *Treating Obsessive Compulsive Disorders*. New York: Pergamon.

Ugazio, V. (1991). La costruzione relazionale dell'organizzazione fobica (The relational construction of phobic organization). In *Dall'individuo al Sistema*, ed. M. Malagoli-Togliatti, and U. Telfener. Turin: Boringhieri.

Varela, F. (1975). A calculus for self-reference. *International Journal of General Systems* 2:5–24.

––––––– (1979). *Principles of Biological Autonomy*. New York: North Holland.

———— (1984). Il circolo creativo: abbozzo di una storia naturale della circolarità. In *The Invented Reality*, ed. P. Watzlawick. New York: Norton.

Watzlawick, P. (1977). *Die Moglichkeit der Anderssein: zur Technick der therapeuischen Kommunikation*. Bern: Heinz Huber.

———— (1985). Hypnotherapy without trance. In *Ericksonian Psychotherapy*, vol. 1, *Structure*, ed. J. Zeig. New York: Brunner/Mazel.

————, ed. (1984). *The Invented Reality*. New York: Norton.

Watzlawick, P., Beavin, J., and Jackson, D. D. (1967). *Pragmatics of Human Communication: A Study on Interactional Patterns, Pathologies and Paradoxes*. New York: Norton.

Watzlawick, P., and Weakland, J. H., eds. (1977). *The Interactional View*. New York: Norton.

Watzlawick, P., Weakland, J. H., and Fisch, R. (1974). *Change: Principles of Problem Formation and Problem Solution*. New York: Norton.

Weakland, J. H., Fisch, R., Watzlawick, P., and Bodin, A. (1974). Brief therapy: focused problem resolution. *Family Process* 13:141–168.

Weeks, G., and L'Abate, L. (1982). *Paradoxical Psychotherapy: Theory and Practice with Individuals, Couple and Family*. New York: Brunner/Mazel.

Wester, W. C., and Smith, H. A. (1984). *Clinical Hypnosis*. Philadelphia: Lippincott.

Whitehead, A. N., and Russell, B. (1910–1913). *Principia Mathematica*. Cambridge, England: Cambridge University Press.

Wiener, N. (1947). Time, communications, and the nervous system. In *Teleological Mechanisms* (Annals of the New York Academy of Sciences), vol. 50, ed. R. W. Miner. Cambridge, MA: Massachusetts Institute of Technology Press, 1948.

———— (1967). *The Human Use of Human Beings: Cybernetics and Society*, 2nd ed. New York: Avon.

———— (1975). *Cybernetics, or Control and Communication in the Animal and the Machine*, 2nd ed. Cambridge, MA: Massachussetts Institute of Technology Press.

Wilde, O. (1986). *Aforismi*. Milan: Mondadori.

Wittgenstein, L. (1914–1916). *Tractatus Logico-Philosophicus e Quaderni 1914–1916*. Turin: Einaudi, 1983.

———— (1933). *Osservazioni sulla Filosofia della Psicologia* (*Remarks on the Philosophy of Psychology*). Milan: Adelphi.

Wolpe, J. (1958). *Psychotherapy by Reciprocal Inhibition*. Stanford, CA: Stanford University Press.

———— (1973). *The Practice of Behavior Therapy*. New York: Pergamon.

———— (1981). *Life Without Fear*. Oakland: New Horlinger.

Zeig, J. (1980). *A Teaching Seminar with Milton J. Erickson*. New York: Brunner/Mazel.

———— (1985). *Ericksonian Psychotherapy*. New York: Brunner/Mazel.

———— (1987). *The Evolution of Psychotherapy*. New York: Brunner/Mazel.

———— (1992). *The Evolution of Psychotherapy: The Second Conference*. New York: Brunner/Mazel.

Index